MOSES

Mark E. Petersen

MOSES
Man of miracles

Deseret Book Company
Salt Lake City, Utah
1977

Library of Congress Cataloging in Publication Data

Petersen, Mark E
   Moses : man of miracles.

   Includes index.
   1. Moses. 2. Mormons and Mormonism—Doctrinal and
controversial works. 3. Bible. O. T.—Biography.
BS580.M6P445   222'.1'0924 [B]   77-21553
ISBN 0-87747-651-9

CONTENTS

PREFACE

Destructive criticism of the Bible, with its companion process of downgrading biblical personalities, has been engaged in over the years. Because of its apparent scholarship, this criticism has led many believers astray, destroying their faith.

Much of the adverse criticism now has been overcome by modern scientific research, including extensive archaeological discoveries. New knowledge has been brought forth to establish the truth of the biblical record.

But revelation is preferred above research. It gives the certain word of God. Modern scripture, received through the Prophet Joseph Smith, completely corroborates the Bible in its many facets, one of which is the certainty of the Israelitish experience in Egypt.

Joseph was sold into bondage. Jacob did take his family to dwell in Egypt in the way the ancient scripture explains. And Moses most certainly led the tribes of Israel back to the Promised Land, with a great display of divine power.

It is to further establish the fact of these important events, in the light of modern revelation, that this book was written.

Chapter 1

MODERN MYTHS AND ANCIENT FACTS

Archaeology has exploded many of the modern myths about ancient man. One of the great delusions has been that ancient peoples lived in deep ignorance and that their intelligence was only a little above the animal level.

It is refreshing to learn now that many of the ancients were very bright people indeed, in some respects equal or superior to many of us who live today.

Caveman stories and the pre-man tales are fast being swept under the rug where they belong as the "diggers for facts" ply their trade. Similar disrepute is likewise coming to the so-called scholarly claims that the Bible is but a collection of legends to be taken only lightly, if at all.

Archaeology is reversing much of this. Already it has blown away much conjecture and supposition and now has unveiled data about the ancient past that help us to turn from fancy to fact and from uncertainty to definite history.

As Sir Charles Marston, noted British researcher, said so effectively in his book *The Bible Comes Alive:*

The effect of these discoveries is to further discredit the whole process of destructive criticism. Archaeology, a strictly objective science, is disproving the subjective negations spun from the mentality of critics.

Those who have shaken popular faith in the Bible, and undermined its authority, are in turn undermined themselves by the evidence that has been brought to light, and their authority destroyed.

The spade is driving destructive criticism out of the field of questionable facts into that of recognized fiction. And it is pretty certain that the process will continue.

Because the early Hebrew scripts had not been discovered in the past, was no evidence at all that they did not exist. Now the Lachish excavations have proved that they did.

Because the background of the Mosaic legislation seemed to fit the end of the Judean monarchy, was no evidence at all that the days of Moses did not fit it even better.

The Ras Shamra tablets, the Semitic legislation of Hammurabi, the Egyptian moral code, the system of worship at Serabit in Sinai, all bear witness that they did. Such shattering discoveries must tend to disillusion those who have had confidence in the soundness of the critical system.

They will begin to recognize the extravagance of its underlying assumption, that *what the critic did not know could not have been.* And how the apparatus of criticism placed a premium on the critic's own ignorance! (London, Edinburgh, and New York: Fleming H. Revell, 1937, pp. 181-82. Italics in original.)

This is strong language, but it comes from a person who is one of the most respected of all the Bible archaeologists. Sir Charles has spent years in Palestinian research and was one of the leaders of the excavations at Lachish. He is well-known on both sides of the Atlantic, having made numerous trips from Britain to the United States in the interest of his diggings in the Holy Land.

On the subject of the Bible critics he continues:

It is surely time that distinguished scholars gave up the habit of representing exploded theories as historical facts. Even they cannot afford to treat Evidence advanced through the Sciences of Archaeology and Anthropology as beneath their notice.

The study of all Religion, which now has been placed on a sound basis by these discoveries, is having further light thrown upon it by other Sciences to which references have been made. (*The Bible Comes Alive*, p. 182.)

In this same vein Will Durant thoughtfully said:

We do not know the whole of man's history; there were probably many civilizations before the Sumerian or the Egyptian; we have just begun to dig! We must operate with partial knowledge, and be provisionally content with probabilities; in history, as in science and politics, relativity rules, and all formulas should be suspect. (*The Lessons of History*, New York: Simon and Schuster, 1968, p. 13.)

In other words, those ancient peoples were not living in any dark ages whether in the Old World or the New, and certainly they were not just emerging from the caveman status either, not by any means! The ancients were highly intelligent, and that includes the Bible patriarchs.

Through the discovery of Ur of the Chaldees by archaeologists, we learn that the people of Abraham's day were well educated, and that instead of living in poverty or being a tent-dwelling people, they were prosperous and had well-built and in some instances luxurious masonry homes in well-planned cities.

For a long time no one knew where Ur of the Chaldees was located; hence some even doubted its existence. Then this ancient city was found by accident and has yielded rich treasures to archaeologists.

The location of ancient Ninevah was found at about the same time, and with it a library of some 20,000 volumes, which shed similar light upon the well-civilized people in that great city. They were wicked, it is true, as is the case with many in other civilized communities, including some of our own, but God loved them enough to send Jonah the prophet to call them to repentance, and they were wise enough to respond.

Keller says that 1500 years before the time of Nebuchadnezzar, the people of Ur were living in spacious two-story homes, some of them having as many as fourteen rooms. Then can anyone say that they were a backward people? And yet they were "early men."

Sir Charles Leonard Woolley, another noted British archaeologist, suggests in his book *Ur Excavations* that since Abraham was born in Ur, he probably was reared in one of those patrician homes and likely grew up in sophisticated surroundings. The houses, Woolley said, reveal comfort and luxury. In them also were found copies of hymns used in temple worship, as well as mathematical tables that used both cube and square root.

Biblical critics have downgraded Abraham as a desert nomad. Did they not know that when he went to the land of Canaan he could not take a patrician two-story masonry home with him from Ur, and thus he had to live in a tent en route? Every evidence from archaeology indicates that Abraham came from a highly civilized community, and that he must have been a product of that kind of life.

Mari, another community of Abraham's day, was an ancient city of high attainment. In one palace area, 1600 cuneiform tablets have been found, detailing items of management. In another area 13,000 clay tablets were found, and in yet another, 8,000. Does that indicate illiteracy? And yet that was more than 2,000 years before the birth of Christ! These also were "early men."

The city of Mari was on the west bank of the Euphrates, some 300 miles upstream from Babylon. Some 200 miles below Babylon lay Ur of the Chaldees. Abraham was reared in an important part of the Fertile Crescent, which was well advanced in culture. But it was an idolatrous land, filled with sin, and the Lord decided to remove Abraham to Canaan.

Canaan was sinful also. However, the Lord determined to cleanse the land by destroying the people living there as he did at Sodom and Gomorrah, for the Canaanites were depraved as were the dwellers in those cities of the plains. Hence the Lord's command to Joshua to wipe them out.

Through the discovery of ancient libraries in Nineveh, Egypt, Palestine, and Mesopotamia in the Eastern Hemisphere, and the unveiling of the accomplishments of the Incas, the Mayas, and the Aztecs in the Western Hemisphere, we now discover a high degree of intelligence among ancient peoples on both sides of the Atlantic that is little short of astonishing.

Achievement in writing, engineering, medicine, astronomy, and mathematics are most noteworthy. The ancients were great builders and they had modern ideas. Is it not interesting, for example, that not only did they build great temples, but that 4,000 years ago people had the convenience of well-planned bathrooms and flush toilets, and living rooms that were spacious and well furnished? Business flourished then, also, even on an international scale. Obviously, then, two to three thousand years before Christ the Fertile Crescent and Egypt had highly developed civilizations.

Ancient Americans also were so well developed in their own day that writers now seem astonished at what they knew and what they did. For example, Dr. Alfred V. Kidder writes, in *A Guide to Quirigua* (page 3), an ancient Mayan city:

The great cities of the Old Maya Empire were built during the first part of the Christian era. For nearly six hundred years these gifted people were leaders in art and architecture, mathematics and astronomy. They evolved a calendar in some ways more accurate than ours.

These artistic and intellectual achievements of the Maya marked the high point in the American Indians' gradual upward progress. The growth of the Indian civilizations, although differing in detail, was strikingly like that of our own, which originated in Egypt and Mesopotamia. . . . Many other resemblances have led some to believe that American civilization was derived from overseas.

Joaquin Munoz, in his small book *The Marvels of Copan,* wrote:

The Maya City of Copan that we now know was not inhabited by savages as early historians thought. Nowhere have savages ever conceived such wonders. . . . Architecture, astronomy, mathematics, painting, weaving, and all the arts that embellish life, once flourished here. Glory, ambition, beauty, warriors, orators, and statesmen lived and passed away and no one knew that such things had ever been. . . .

With their calendrical system in perfect order, the Maya appear on the threshold of history 600 years before the Christian era, and among their first great cities was Copan where building in stone reached its highest development. Scientists and artists are everywhere of the opinion that the sculptures and the arts of the Maya deserve to rank among the finest in the world. Modern astronomers marvel at the progress made by this people in the measuring of time by observed movements of the heavenly bodies. (Pages 13, 14-15.)

"Six centuries before Christ, before the Persian wars and the Great Golden age of Athens, the Indians of Oaxaca had already worked out a calendar," says Helen Augur. (*The Zapotecs,* p. 126).

Some scholars have felt that the ancient Americans had no steel, iron, or any hard tools other than stone. We have this from A. Hyatt Verrill in his *America's Ancient Civilizations:*

Can anyone actually believe, as archaeologists claim, that the colossal work [of leveling off a mountain at Monte Alban] was accomplished with crude stone implements and that the broken rock was transported in baskets carried on human heads? No one with an atom of common sense and a smattering of knowledge of engineering problems can actually believe that the Zapotecs cut away hundreds of thousands of tons of rock, filled yawning ravines and deep fissures with rubble, leveled an area hundreds of acres in extent and built huge, imposing structures all with no knowledge of steel tools, no explosives, no wheeled vehicles and no beasts of burden.

Book of Mormon readers of course know that both the Jaredites and the Nephites used steel, and had common use of the wheel. Regarding the Jaredites we read:

And they did work in all manner of ore, and they did make gold, and silver, and iron, and brass, and all manner of metals; and they did dig it out of the earth; wherefore they did cast up mighty heaps of earth to get ore, of gold, and of silver, and of iron, and of copper. And they did work all manner of fine work.

And they did make all manner of tools to till the earth, both to plow and to sow, to reap and to hoe, and also to thrash.

And they did make all manner of tools with which they did work their beasts. (Ether 10:23, 25-26.)

The Nephites did likewise:

And I, Nephi, did take the sword of Laban, and after the manner of it did make many swords, lest by any means the people who were now called Lamanites should come upon us and destroy us; for I knew their hatred towards me and my children and those who were called my people.

And I did teach my people to build buildings, and to work in all manner of wood, and of iron, and of copper, and of brass, and of steel, and of gold, and of silver, and of precious ores, which were in great abundance. (2 Nephi 5:14-15.)

In *The American Book of Indians* we find this statement: "The Mayas attained the highest civilization known in ancient America and one of the highest known any place in the early world." (New York: American Heritage Publishing Co., p. 19.) The book then comments on the excellence of the Mayan written language.

A remarkable book is Werner Keller's *The Bible As History,* in which the author lifts the curtain on the ancient Fertile Crescent where "Egypt's mighty pyramids and Mesopotamia's massive temples have for centuries watched the busy life around them." This was 2500 years before Christ!

The author says that the highly developed civilizations there "jostled each other in colorful and bewildering array. . . . the art of cuneiform and hieroglyphic writing was commonly known. Poets, court officials, and civil servants practiced it. For commerce it had long been a necessity.

Literature and learning were flourishing. In Egypt the first novels and secular poetry were making their appearance. Mesopotamia was experiencing a renaissance. Philologists in Akkad, the great kingdom on the lower Euphrates, were compiling the first grammar and the first bilingual dictionary.

The story of Gilgamesh, and the old Sumerian legends of creation and flood were being woven into epics of dramatic power in the Akkadian tongue which was the language of the world. Egyptian doctors were producing their medicines in accordance with textbook methods from herbal compounds that had proved their worth. Their surgeons were no strangers to anatomical science.

By empirical means the mathematicians of the Nile reached the con-
clusion about the sides of a right-angled triangle which fifteen hundred
years later Pythagoras in Greece embodied in the theorem which bears his
name. (New York: William Morrow and Co., pp. 4, 5-6.)

He goes on to extoll the highly developed skills of the
ancient construction engineers and especially the accuracy of
the astronomers who made such precise calculations from
their study of the stars.

About 1700 B.C. Mari was razed by Hammurabi of
Babylon, and it was never rebuilt. Some of the ruins of the
palace of King Zimrilim, the last ruler of Mari, have been
excavated. Some walls 16 feet high, well preserved by the
desert sands, were found there. Mural paintings were uncovered with their colors hardly affected by time. Archaeologists found 20,000 clay tablets with texts in Babylonian
cuneiform. On some of them biblical names appear.

The *New Atlas of the Bible* (New York: Doubleday, 1969,
p. 41) indicates that the high culture of Mari was "common
property" in those days, thus illustrating still further the advanced state of those people. And Abraham was one of
them.

Craftsmen were well trained and had guilds or unions
even in that day. On some tablets were found the names of
as many as 2,000 such craftsmen, each one listed by name
and guild.

So were the people in the time of the patriarchs ignorant
and illiterate, or were they mere desert nomads?

To say that men like Abraham and Moses were not able
to produce the kind of writing that we now know they did
produce, and to say that such men knew nothing of
astronomy, into which they delved deeply, is to totally ignore
the facts.

Not only were they a part of the culture in which they
lived, and therefore were educated by it, but they also had
further and vastly superior instruction, for Almighty God
was their teacher. Who but the Creator could discuss
astronomy, for example, with such complete accuracy? In
literal fact, it was the Creator who taught those early men,
beginning with Adam. Ignorance certainly was not a part of
their lives.

The Cradle of Civilization boldly declares that "no civilization existed anywhere on the earth's surface before 3,000 B.C." (New York: Time-Life Books, Inc., 1967, p. 7.) This speculative declaration, of course, ignores scripture which shows that well before then, Adam and his family were highly civilized, having been taught by God himself.

This same book (page 12) speaks of Sumerian temples built on a grand scale and dating "from as early as 3,000 B.C." Ruins of those temples have yielded hundreds of clay tablets, while from nearby buildings and cemeteries still other tablets have come showing the high intellectual development of those people. In another chapter in the book we read that man learned to enjoy leisure and the sedentary life as early as 10,000 years ago. Isn't it interesting how writers vary in their dating efforts, even within the covers of the same book?

The *New Atlas of the Bible* reports that civilization emerged in the Fertile Crescent area by 4500 B.C., but adds that the art of writing did not develop for another thousand years. (New York: Doubleday, 1969, pp. 27-32.) This too is based on conjecture from what archaeologists have found there. Who knows but that new finds will change their minds again, as Sir Charles Marston so emphatically said?

Efforts to place early man as far back as 30,000 or 50,000 or 100,000 years are but bald speculation, of course. The manner in which dating methods, and particularly the C-14 method, are presently being challenged is significant in this regard.

When did civilization start?

It began with Adam, the first man, unusually well educated because the Lord was his teacher. (Moses 6.) It is admitted that there was retrogression among some of his family who apostatized and then left his well-ordered society. They were the backsliders who left the true faith and culture of Adam and the patriarchs and sank so low that they became carnal, sensual, and devilish.

"And Satan came among them, saying: I am also a son of God; and he commanded them, saying: Believe it not; and they believed it not, and they loved Satan more than

God. *And men began from that time forth to be carnal, sensual, and devilish."* (Moses 5:13. See also D&C 20:20.)

Thus they became the cavemen and other early degenerates who some scholars now mistakenly believe were the first men.

All of this differs but little from situations found among certain aborigines who live today in some parts of the world. Both the caveman-type and the advanced man of our present culture still live today, as examples of the contrast between human retrogression on one hand and cultural advancement on the other.

Since this is happening today, can anyone say that the condition did not also exist 5,000 or 6,000 years ago?

Carleton S. Coon has written:

> Many peoples were still in the Stone Age when Europeans began their voyages of exploration and discovery in the A.D. 1400s. The aborigines of Tasmania and Australia were using techniques of the Old Stone Age when white men discovered them in the 1700's. White men found the African Bushmen living in the Middle Stone Age. Islanders of the South Pacific Ocean and most American Indians had progressed to the New Stone Age. A few tribes in New Guinea and Australia are still in the Stone Age. (*The World Book Encyclopedia* 18:714.)

The United Press International on Wednesday, May 19, 1976, carried a dispatch from Lima, Peru, concerning so-called Stone Age natives presently living in the jungles of that country. They were described as hunchbacked men more than six feet six inches tall. "The giants have been reported only in the San Martin Province, an area of thick rain forests and wooded foothills east of the Andes," said the dispatch.

> Carlos Torrealza, discoverer of the ruins of a lost Indian city in San Martin Province said he came across the giants while lost for two weeks in the jungle. Clad only in animal skins, with reddish hair, and speaking a dialect he had never heard, they fled at his approach, he said.
> Days later two large circulation Lima newspapers, Ultina Hora and La Prensa quoted an Indian guide, Encarnacion Napuri, as saying that on April 26 a group of about fifteen giant aborigines armed with thick wooden clubs, stone-headed axes, and hardwood lances attacked a camp of professional hunters. . . .
> He said the giants may be descended from the Chancas, a tribe that retreated into the northern jungles rather than submit to the Spanish conquistadores.

In 1971 several newspaper articles, with pictures, appeared in America telling of some Stone Age people found in the Tasaday Forest area of the Philippine Islands during March of that year. John Nance, Associated Press writer, described them as "the gentle people of this rain forest."

Concerning these people, the *Deseret News* of July 21, 1971, quoted a United Press International dispatch as follows: "A tribe living in Stone Age culture, in a tropical rain forest, isolated from the rest of the world for perhaps 2,000 years, has something the civilized world seems to have lost along the centuries—sound teeth."

Anthropologists and newsmen visited this tribe and said their tools and technology were more primitive than the Negritoes, who were described in the dispatch as a post-Stone Age tribe living on Luzon Island. Colonel Charles A. Lindbergh assisted in this study.

The dispatch continued: "The Tasadays are purely food-gathering and animal-trapping forest people, without agriculture or a way of slaying an animal, according to Dr. Frank Lynch, an Irish anthropologist now with the Ajeneo University in Manila. They have never known sugar, rice, tobacco or salt."

The dispatch goes on at length. But the point is that there are still living in the world peoples who are said by anthropologists to be of Stone Age culture.

The Kansas City *Times* on November 28, 1975, carried a New York Times News Service article by Boyce Rensberger stating that scientists have now changed their minds about the Neanderthal man, the allegedly "hulking brutish creature of 60,000 years ago." They now have decided that he was intelligent after all, and that he knew something about medicine; in fact, he knew about seven different species of medicinal herbs. Of course the dating is still subject to much revision.

In the London *Daily Telegraph* of June 19, 1976, is a photograph of Egyptologist Dr. Rosaline David taking fingerprints and toeprints of an Egyptian female mummy five feet tall. The prints confirmed, said the newspaper, "that she had done very little housework. The hands of many modern housewives would be in much worse condition. We guess that she was about 40 years old when she died." The mummy was believed to be that of a dancer who lived 3500 years ago. There was nothing "cave-womanish" about her!

In the London *Daily Times* of June 13, 1976, another archaeology story appeared on the front page. Dr. Shmed Moussa, inspector of antiquities of Saqqara, near Cairo, Egypt, had discovered the "beautiful and intact mummy of a singer named Waty who died 4,348 years ago, a full 500 years before the oldest intact mummy previously discovered. He is a unique survivor of the Old Kingdom of Egypt."

Pictures were taken "and the result is an extraordinary view of man as he was more than four millennia ago." The *Times* published the picture in color, and his body was not different from ours!

A musician, 4,348 years ago? A singer? Who taught him to sing? Moses also sang as he left Egypt a thousand years later.

Research constantly demonstrates that the ancients were highly intelligent, well-educated, and far from the types that certain anthropologists parade as early men.

When Professor A. H. Sayer wrote about developments in Egypt, he said:

> The earliest culture and civilization to which monuments bear witness was in fact already perfect. It was full grown. The organization of the country was complete. The arts were known and practiced. Egyptian culture as far as we know at present has no beginnings. . . . The older the culture the more perfect it is found to be. (Hilbricht, *Recent Researches in Bible Lands,* pp. 101-2.)

Opinions on the origin of language are also changing. Otto Jesperson, in his book *Language, Its Nature, Development and Origin,* said:

> We find that the ancient languages of our family, Sanscrit, Zend, etc., abound in very long words; the further back we go, the greater the number of sesquipedalia. We have seen also how the current theory, according to which every language started with monosyllabic roots [or grunts], fails at every point to account for actual fact, and breaks down before the established truth of linguistic history. (New York: Henry Holt and Co., 1922, p. 420.)

Although some fell away and regressed, ancient men

were generally intelligent and enjoyed a high degree of civilization.

But why do we write all of this? Simply to establish that Moses and his divinely chosen predecessors—the patriarchs—were not of the caveman class by any means, but rather were fully qualified to teach great truths as they did.

Furthermore, as servants of God they had the gift of the Holy Ghost, and under the influence of that divine Spirit they were far better prepared to write historical facts and inspirational matter than were any of the Egyptians, the Sumerians, or others of those early days.

The following scripture from the Book of Moses is especially enlightening in this regard:

> And a book of remembrance was kept, in the which was recorded, in the language of Adam, for it was given unto as many as called upon God to write by the spirit of inspiration;
> And by them their children were taught to read and write, having a language which was pure and undefiled. (Moses 6:5-6.)

Taught as they were by the Lord himself, and having the advantage of a civilized background such as archaeology now reveals, our early prophets and patriarchs were well equipped for their work. We have every reason to have full and complete confidence in what they taught as we study their writings in the scriptures.

Chapter 2

MOSES WAS A REALITY

The prophet Moses was a reality.

He was one of the mightiest men who ever lived. He was a prophet of God without parallel, a man whose work had both ancient and modern significance.

With the possible exception of the Prophet Joseph Smith, Abraham, Enoch, and the brother of Jared, Moses appears to have had a closer personal relationship with the Almighty than any other man of whom we know.

He saw the Lord repeatedly, walked and talked with him frequently; for a time he experienced heavenly glory although still in mortality, and he was called—by the Deity himself—a son of God.

What though the myth-makers downgrade him, even call his work a legend! What though they attempt to rob him of the authorship of his books in the Bible and discount the inspiration of the Ten Commandments, even attributing them to other ancient peoples!

Modern revelation shows Moses to have been one of the outstanding prophets of all time, and establishes beyond question that he did write the books of the Bible credited to him, that he did receive the Decalogue from the Lord, personally, and that he did lead Israel out of Egypt under divine direction, regardless of all that the scholarly critics might say.

See at a glance what the scriptures tell of him:

He was called to the work by the personal visitation and direct voice of the Lord. (Exodus 3:4.)

At one time heavenly glory came upon him and he was able to endure it. (Moses 1:1-31.)

He walked and talked with God as did Enoch. (Moses 1:1-42.)

He was described by the Deity as being "in the similitude of [the] Only Begotten." (Moses 1:6.)

He beheld in vision the creations of God. (Moses 1:4, 8; 2:1.)

He beheld this entire world and all of its inhabitants, this too in glorious vision. (Moses 1:28.)

He battled Satan face to face—and won! (Moses 1:12-22.)

He saw in vision the bitterness of hell. (Moses 1:20.)

He delivered Israel from bondage. (Exodus 12-14.)

He received the tablets of the Decalogue from the Lord (Deuteronomy 10), and the Book of Mormon tells us that it was Jesus Christ, as Jehovah, who gave him the law which in turn he gave to Israel. (3 Nephi 15.)

He wrote Genesis and other books of the Bible. (1 Nephi 5:11-14.)

He ministered to the Lord Jesus Christ on the Mount of Transfiguration, thus giving further testimony of the divinity of Jesus. (Matthew 17:1-3.)

He played an important part in the modern restoration of the gospel by coming to Joseph Smith in the Kirtland Temple. There he delivered to the modern prophet the keys of the gathering of Israel, that all Israel might be reassembled in the last days, which is to be one of the major events to transpire in the hour of God's judgment. (D&C 110.)

When he finished his mortal work he was taken unto God, as is indicated both in the Book of Mormon and in ancient Jewish writings.

Moses was spoken of frequently by the Savior during the Lord's earthly ministry. There was no doubt in the Savior's mind that Moses was the great lawgiver of ancient times, for it was the Savior himself who, as the God of the Old Testament, dealt with him. (3 Nephi 15.)

Testimony of the great lawgiver is provided in all the scriptures: the Bible, the Book of Mormon, the Doctrine and Covenants, and the Pearl of Great Price. It appears frequently also in the teachings of the modern prophets.

Moses indeed was a great reality, and a study of his life and labors is an inspiring experience.

He was in fact raised up by the Almighty for the express purpose of releasing Israel from Egypt whence they had gone for food more than four hundred years earlier.

It was his responsibility and honor to lead them back to their promised land of Palestine, to free them from bondage in Egypt, and to teach them obedience to the true and living God.

Chapter 3

ISRAEL IN EGYPT

Many scholars ridicule the story of Joseph being sold into Egypt and of Jacob and his family coming later, taking up a new home in Goshen.

They call attention to the complete silence of Egyptian records regarding the story of Israel in Egypt—silence for the 430 years during which the Bible says Jacob's descendants lived there.

If the Israelites really were in Egypt, why do not the voluminous records kept by the Egyptians give them even a casual mention?

As one competent writer said:

> No country in the ancient East has handed down its history so faithfully as Egypt. Right back to about 3,000 B.C. we can trace the names of the Pharaohs practically without a break. We know the succession of dynasties in the Old, Middle, and New Kingdoms. No other people have recorded so meticulously their important events . . . the erection of temples and palaces, as well as their literature and poetry.
>
> But this time Egypt gave the scholars no answer. As if it were not enough that they found nothing about Joseph, they discovered neither documents nor monuments out of this whole period. (Keller, *The Bible As History*, p. 86.)

The story of Joseph's encounter with Potipher's wife is alleged by critics to have been a purloined version of "The Tale of the Two Brothers," which was deciphered from hieroglyphics of the XIX Dynasty period and which told a somewhat similar story.

Joseph isn't mentioned in Egytian records, the scholars say. Was his whole story but a legend, then, not worthy of being inscribed in stone as were other important events? Wasn't Joseph really the viceroy of all Egypt? Did he not in fact save the nation from starvation? Is history to be silent forever on the subject?

We know from revelation, modern and ancient, that the story of Joseph's capture and banishment into Egypt is true. Then why does not Egyptian history corroborate the Bible account, since it is so important?

The reason is clear and adequate.

The year 1730 B.C. was a fateful one for Egypt. It was then that the land was invaded by a people known as the Hyksos, a Semitic tribe from Canaan and Syria. They shattered the Middle Kingdom of the Egyptians, seized the entire country, set up their own domineering rule, made their own pharaohs, and ruled with an iron hand.

The name Hyksos was derived from the definition "rulers from foreign lands." And so they were. Their cruel treatment of the Egyptians bred a severe hatred in the hearts of the populace, so that by the time the Hyksos were driven from the country some two hundred years later, the Egyptians were anxious to forget all about them, and erased mention of them from most of their records and monuments. Hence no record of Joseph, who was contemporary with the Hyksos.

Keep in mind that the Hyksos were Semites. The Israelites also were Semites. There was no Egyptian blood in either group. Then would the Egyptian historians have extolled the Israelites or Joseph?

According to the best estimates of the Bible scholars, it was about the year 1700 B.C. that Joseph was sold into Egypt. He came into a Semite-controlled government. He himself was a Semite. Historians believe that this fact was partially responsible for the recognition he received from the Semite-Hyksos pharaoh. He was regarded in a sense as a blood brother, held captive in a foreign land.

As Keller expresses it:

Under the Pharaohs a sand-dweller [such as Joseph] could never have become viceroy. Nomads bred asses, sheep and goats and the Egyptians despised none so much as breeders of small cattle, "For every shepherd is an abomination unto the Egyptians." (Gen. 46:34.)

Only under the foreign overlords, the Hyksos, would an Asiatic have the chance to rise to the highest office in the state. Under the Hyksos we repeatedly find officials with Semitic names. On scarabs dating from the Hyksos period the name "Jacob-Her," has been clearly deciphered.

"And it is not impossible," concludes the great American Egyptologist James Henry Breasted, "that a leader of the Israelite tribe of Jacob gained control for a time in the Nile valley in this obscure period. Such an occurrence would fit in surprisingly well with the migration to Egypt of Israelite tribes which in any case must have taken place about this time." (*The Bible as History,* p. 93.)

It is of importance to note that Joseph married Asenath, a Semite girl of the Hyksos tribe and a daughter of Potipherah, a priest in the Hyksos regime. Therefore, she was not of Egyptian blood, but Semite. Joseph also was a Semite, so he married within his own race.

The pharaoh of this period, it will be remembered, was exceptionally kind to Jacob, the father of Joseph, and to Jacob's entire family. He gave them one of his choice agricultural areas, Goshen, where they grew and thrived.

The pharaoh's great kindness to Jacob may also be related to the fact that Jacob was a Semite in a foreign land, as of course was his son Joseph. It is therefore not to be wondered at that pharaoh would authorize an expensive funeral procession back to Semite Palestine where the Semite Jacob was to be buried. Jacob is believed to have died about 1689 B.C. This was some forty years after the invasion by the Hyksos and about ten years after the arrival of Joseph in Egypt.

The Bible speaks of one pharaoh "who knew not Joseph." This is an interesting commentary, and it is related to an important event in Egyptian history.

In 1567 B.C. one of the weak regional rulers, Ahmosis, an Egyptian vassal king who had been tolerated by the Hyksos because of his supposed weakness, began a war of liberation. So great was the hatred of the populace toward the Hyksos, and so universally did they respond to the attempt at liberation, that they united in a mighty effort that eventually drove the Hyksos out of the country.

This gave rise to the XVIII Dynasty and what is known as the New Kingdom. A revived spirit of liberation and hope swept through Egypt. All thought of further submission to any foreign power was gone. Native Egyptian pharaohs now came into power; and one of them, the great Thutmosis III, determined, as we would say in our day, that the best defense is a strong offense. He thereupon decided to conquer the world and nearly did so. His armies drove through Palestine, beyond the great bend in the Euphrates, and over-ran Syria. By the time Amenophis III came to the throne, Egypt was dominant in that entire portion of the world. It was into such an age that Moses was born.

These new pharaohs, wholly Egyptian and completely hateful toward the Semite Hyksos, and all Semites for that matter, were the pharaohs that "knew not Joseph." It was by them that the Israelites—"alien" Semites that they were—had been placed under bondage.

Chapter 4

THE SILENT PERIOD

Although Egyptian records are silent concerning the Egyptian residency of the Israelites, some evidences of their being there are nevertheless known.

To obtain a clear picture of the situation, of course, we must go to the scriptures, which give abundant information, with modern revelation corroborating the Bible account, thereby making the narrative fully acceptable.

It is important that we have an understanding of the probable time when these things took place. No specific dates can be found, but by fitting events together in the known time frames, it is possible to arrive at fairly close estimates.

As has been indicated, the Hyksos invaded Egypt in or about 1730 B.C.

Joseph is believed to have been sold into Egypt about 1700 B.C. His father, Jacob, died in Egypt probably about 1689 B.C.

The Bible indicates that the Israelites were in Egypt for 430 years. Counting from the time Joseph came to that land, in approximately 1700, and deducting the 430 years of their residence there, we come near to 1270 B.C. as the possible time of their liberation.

It is fairly well established that Ramses II came to the throne in 1301. Some believe he was the pharaoh of the enslavement.

Ramses' successor is believed to have been Meneptah II, and it is conjectured that this Meneptah was the pharaoh of the exodus.

Ramses was an egotistical monarch who took it upon himself to erase from public buildings and monuments all names that were distasteful to him and then to replace them with his own. Naturally any reference to the Hyksos suffered. Again, we see why there are few records of this dark period.

Ramses had a passion for building and then placing his name upon every structure he erected. He catered to his insatiable ego also, as he placed his name on monuments and buildings others had erected, in some cases hundreds of years before.

This extensive building required much work, and slave labor was cheap. The Israelites were within easy reach, so they were forced into slavery for construction purposes.

It is this that provides some evidence of Israelite residency there. For example, one of the large funeral murals found by archaeologists shows dark-skinned men driving enslaved white men in making and laying bricks.

Semites were white people. The Israelites, being Semites themselves, were also white. They were the slaves. The native dark-skinned Egyptians were the taskmasters. The mural is dated at the approximate period of the enslavement.

Keller makes an interesting comment on this point:

The painting in the rock tomb shows a scene from the building of the Temple of Amun in Thebes. The classical bond cities of the children of Israel were, however, Pithom and Raamses. Both names appear in slightly different form in Egyptian inventories.

"Pi-Tum," "House of the god Tum"—is a town which was built by Ramesses II. Pi-Ramses-Meri-Amun which has already been mentioned, is the Biblical Raamses. An inscription of the time of Ramesses II speaks of "PR, who hauled the stones for the great fortress of the city of Pi-Ramses-Meri-Amun." "PR" is Egyptian hieroglyphics for Semites. (*The Bible as History*, p. 118.)

So the pharaohs who "knew not Joseph," and who turned against the Israelites and enslaved them, were true Egyptians, once again on the throne, fully free from Hyksos influence. It was these pharaohs who feared the prolific Hebrews and who felt that slavery was the means by which they could control them best and thus prevent them from gaining power in the government.

The Bible Companion explains it this way:

The new pharaoh, who was not a Semite Hyksos, but a native Egyptian, took no account of the service which Joseph had done to his country and was afraid that, with the Hebrew population increasing so swiftly, it might make common cause with the invaders. For the normal route of attack on Egypt was by way of the Delta, the region in which the Hebrews lived. So he put them to hard labour to build store cities. (William Neil, ed., New York: McGraw-Hill, 1960, p. 10.)

Archaeologists point with pride to their discovery of graneries in various parts of Egypt, not unlike the silos that may be seen in rural United States and Canada today. Although smaller, they were efficient in the preservation of grain. There is little doubt that these silos go back to the Hyksos period when Joseph was viceroy of Egypt.

Chapter 5

JOSEPH WAS THERE!

Revelation is more dependable than research, and scripture is more certain than speculative writings in history.

Ancient scripture and modern revelation establish the presence of Joseph in Egypt and the remarkable events of his life. They also make it known that he was a great prophet in those times and that he prophesied concerning our day.

He even made known the calling of the Prophet Joseph Smith, far in advance of the latter's work, and designated his name and the name of the boy prophet's father. He predicted both would be called Joseph, after himself. It is all very remarkable, and a great testimony to the manner in which the Lord directs his affairs here on earth.

The prophet Lehi, in blessing his own son Joseph, said:

> For behold, thou art the fruit of my loins; and I am a descendant of Joseph who was carried captive into Egypt. And great were the covenants of the Lord which he made unto Joseph.
>
> Wherefore, Joseph truly saw our day. And he obtained a promise of the Lord, that out of the fruit of his loins the Lord God would raise up a righteous branch unto the house of Israel; not the Messiah, but a branch which was to be broken off, nevertheless, to be remembered in the covenants of the Lord that the Messiah should be made manifest unto them in the latter days, in the spirit of power, unto the bringing of them out of darkness unto light—yea, out of hidden darkness and out of captivity unto freedom. (2 Nephi 3:4-5.)

It was Lehi who revealed that the ancient Joseph foretold the coming of Joseph Smith, the seer of latter days. Lehi further taught his young son Joseph while in the wilderness:

> For Joseph truly testified, saying: A seer shall the Lord my God raise up, who shall be a choice seer unto the fruit of my loins.
>
> Yea, Joseph truly said: Thus saith the Lord unto me: A choice seer will I raise up out of the fruit of thy loins; and he shall be esteemed highly among the fruit of thy loins. And unto him will I give commandment that he shall do a work for the fruit of thy loins, his brethren, which shall be of

great worth unto them, even to the bringing of them to the knowledge of the covenants which I have made with thy fathers.

And I will give unto him a commandment that he shall do none other work, save the work which I shall command him. And I will make him great in mine eyes; for he shall do my work.

And he shall be great like unto Moses, whom I have said I would raise up unto you, to deliver my people, O house of Israel.

And Moses will I raise up, to deliver thy people out of the land of Egypt.

But a seer will I raise up out of the fruit of thy loins; and unto him will I give power to bring forth my word unto the seed of thy loins—and not to the bringing forth my word only, said the Lord, but to the convincing them of my word, which shall have already gone forth among them.

Wherefore, the fruit of thy loins shall write; and the fruit of the loins of Judah shall write; and that which shall be written by the fruit of thy loins, and also that which shall be written by the fruit of the loins of Judah, shall grow together, unto the confounding of false doctrines and laying down of contentions, and establishing peace among the fruit of thy loins, and bringing them to the knowledge of their fathers in the latter days, and also to the knowledge of my covenants, saith the Lord.

And out of weakness he shall be made strong, in that day when my work shall commence among all my people, unto the restoring thee, O house of Israel, saith the Lord.

And thus prophesied Joseph, saying: Behold, that seer will the Lord bless; and they that seek to destroy him shall be confounded; for this promise, which I have obtained of the Lord, of the fruit of my loins, shall be fulfilled. Behold, I am sure of the fulfilling of this promise;

And his name shall be called after me; and it shall be after the name of his father. And he shall be like unto me; for the thing, which the Lord shall bring forth by his hand, by the power of the Lord shall bring my people unto salvation.

Yea, thus prophesied Joseph: I am sure of this thing, even as I am sure of the promise of Moses; for the Lord hath said unto me, I will preserve thy seed forever. (2 Nephi 3:6-16.)

Because the Book of Mormon is true, the story of Joseph in Egypt is also true. Even though some modern critics discount the event, we know through modern scripture that he was thus sold and that the account of his presence there is true.

When Nephi and his brothers brought the brass plates of Laban to their father,

it came to pass that my father, Lehi, also found upon the plates of brass a genealogy of his fathers; wherefore he knew that he was a descendant of Joseph; yea, *even that Joseph who was the son of Jacob, who was sold into Egypt,* and who was preserved by the hand of the Lord, that he might preserve his father, Jacob, and all his household from perishing with famine.

And they were also led out of captivity and out of the land of Egypt, by that same God who had preserved them.

And thus my father, Lehi, did discover the genealogy of his fathers. And Laban also was a descendant of Joseph, wherefore he and his fathers had kept the records. (1 Nephi 5:14-16. Italics added.)

Again the Book of Mormon confirms the Bible and removes questions and doubts raised by the critics.

But this scripture is not all. Lehi, a descendant of that same Joseph, in giving a reason for his own departure into the wilderness said: "Wherefore, thus saith the Lord, I have led this people forth out of the land of Jerusalem, by the power of mine arm, that I might raise up unto me a righteous branch from the fruit of the loins of Joseph." (Jacob 2:25.)

When Amulek and Alma were making their great defense in the days of Zeezrom, Amulek spoke of his descent from Joseph of Egypt. He testified:

I am Amulek; I am the son of Giddonah, who was the son of Ishmael, who was a descendant of Aminadi; and it was the same Aminadi who interpreted the writing which was upon the wall of the temple, which was witten by the finger of God.

And Aminadi was a descendant of Nephi, who was the son of Lehi, who came out of the land of Jerusalem, who was a descendant of Manasseh, who was the son of *Joseph who was sold into Egypt* by the hands of his brethren. (Alma 10:2-3. Italics added.)

The great general Moroni, who established the banner of liberty among the Nephites, likewise testified of Joseph, saying:

Yea, let us preserve our liberty as a remnant of Joseph; yea, let us remember the words of Jacob, before his death, for behold, he saw that a part of the remnant of the coat of Joseph was preserved and had not decayed. And he said—Even as this remnant of garment of my son hath been preserved, so shall a remnant of the seed of my son be preserved by the hand of God, and be taken unto himself, while the remainder of the seed of Joseph shall perish, even as the remnant of his garment.

Now behold, this giveth my soul sorrow; nevertheless, my soul hath joy in my son, because of that part of his seed which shall be taken unto God.

Now behold, this was the language of Jacob.

And now who knoweth but what the remnant of the seed of Joseph, which shall perish as his garment, are those who have dissented from us? Yea, and even it shall be ourselves if we do not stand fast in the faith of Christ. (Alma 46:24-27.)

In the events leading up to the appearance of the Savior to the Nephites we read: "Behold, our father Jacob also testified concerning a remnant of the seed of Joseph. And behold, are not we a remnant of the seed of Joseph? And these things which testify of us, are they not written upon the plates of brass which our father Lehi brought out of Jerusalem?" (3 Nephi 10:17.)

As he was closing up the record of the Book of Mormon, Moroni added another testimony concerning Joseph in Egypt, this one coming from the prophet Ether:

> Behold, Ether saw the days of Christ, and he spake concerning a New Jerusalem upon this land.
>
> And he spake also concerning the house of Israel, and the Jerusalem from whence Lehi should come—after it should be destroyed it should be built up again, a holy city unto the Lord; wherefore, it could not be a new Jerusalem for it had been in a time of old; but it should be built up again, and become a holy city of the Lord; and it should be built unto the house of Israel.
>
> And that a New Jerusalem should be built upon this land, unto the remnant of the seed of Joseph, for which things there has been a type.
>
> For as *Joseph brought his father down into the land of Egypt,* even so he died there; wherefore, the Lord brought a remnant of the seed of Joseph out of the land of Jerusalem, that he might be merciful unto the seed of Joseph that they should perish not, even as he was merciful unto the father of Joseph that he should perish not.
>
> Wherefore, the remnant of the house of Joseph shall be built upon this land; and it shall be a land of their inheritance; and they shall build up a holy city unto the Lord, like unto the Jerusalem of old; and they shall no more be confounded, until the end come when the earth shall pass away. (Ether 13:4-8. Italics added.)

In modern revelation to the Prophet Joseph Smith the Lord speaks of the promises made to the house of Joseph, this same Joseph who was the son of Jacob, and who was sold into Egypt. For example we have: "Behold, this is the law I gave unto my servant Nephi, and thy fathers, Joseph, and Jacob, and Isaac, and Abraham, and all mine ancient prophets and apostles." (D&C 98:32.)

The house of Joseph is to be convinced of the gospel, as is indicated in this passage: "And then cometh the day when the arm of the Lord shall be revealed in power in convincing the nations, the heathen nations, the house of Joseph, of the gospel of their salvation." (D&C 90:10.)

It is obvious that Joseph was very important to the Lord and that his descendants were to be choice in his sight. Although many may go astray, eventually salvation will come to his house.

Chapter 6

A PURPOSE IN EGYPT

The Lord had a purpose in bringing Jacob and his family into Egypt, and it was far beyond merely saving them from temporary famine.

That dearth was what forced the family to go to Egypt where there was corn, and where the Lord obviously wanted them to be. The famine was his means of bringing them there. In Goshen they could develop into a populous people, which was not possible under the conditions prevailing in Palestine at that period.

We have an interesting parallel to this episode in the early life of the Prophet Joseph Smith. His father was a farmer who was beset constantly by financial reverses. Looking for better farmland, Joseph Smith, Sr., moved his family from place to place until at last he settled near Palmyra, New York.

That is where the Lord wanted him to be—near the Book of Mormon plates in the Hill Cumorah.

This move to the Palmyra area set the stage for the great work of restoration to be accomplished by Joseph Smith, Jr., chosen to be the prophet of latter days. But the Lord used adversity to bring the family to the area where he wished them to be.

So it was with Jacob's family. The Lord used adversity to persuade them to go where he wished them to be.

The fulfillment of God's promises to Abraham required that Israel should become numerous. To accomplish this, the little family, numbering only 70 persons (Genesis 46:26-27), needed sufficient time and a peaceful place in which to grow. Egypt was that place.

The opportunities for development in Palestine in those days were limited indeed. The people were almost wholly pastoral. Jacob's family kept sheep and goats for a living.

Their income was small and so was their influence. Yet their destiny was ultimately to affect the entire world.

Also, Palestine was a battleground for warring nations that moved back and forth in their conquests between the Nile and the Euphrates. Israel would have found no peace there. They required stable conditions for their eventual growth and development. So what did the Lord do?

He took them out of their promised but troubled homeland and sent them into what at first was truly a place of refuge, where comparative peace and plenty awaited them. Goshen was one of the most fertile parts of the entire Nile valley, and of the whole Middle East, for that matter.

The Lord took them to this rich land, too, under the benign rule of a pharaoh who not only knew Joseph, but appreciated him and made the young Hebrew his viceroy.

Their stay in Egypt for 430 years allowed them the time to grow and flourish. It permitted them to become the mighty host that eventually left under Moses, with 600,000 men plus their families.

The Bible says concerning their departure: "And the children of Israel journeyed from Rameses to Succoth, about 600,000 on foot that were men, beside children. And a mixed multitude went up also with them; and flocks, and herds, even very much cattle." (Exodus 12:37-38.)

The modernized Jewish Torah describes it in essentially the same terms: "The Israelites journeyed from Raamses to Succoth, about six hundred thousand men on foot, aside from children. Moreover, a mixed multitude went up with them, and very much livestock, both flocks and herds." (Jewish Publication Society of America, 1962.)

It would be interesting to know the meaning of the "mixed multitude." But there is no explanation.

The 600,000 men, plus their families, would indicate that the entire host must have numbered as many as two or three million, counting wives and children. The Israelites must have numbered in the millions, for at one time they had a standing army of 400,000 "footmen that drew sword." (See Judges 20:2, 17.) The book of Judges also speaks of a battle in which 120,000 "men that drew sword" lost their lives. (Judges 8:10.)

Their bondage certainly was not all on the negative side. It too served a good purpose. The cruelty of the taskmasters, the hatred that existed between the Hebrews and the Egyptians, and the length of their trying servitude fused Jacob's children into a united people.

Stubborn and unbending as they were, could anything else have done it? Only in such a way could twelve independent and bickering tribes have been compelled to adopt one purpose, one hope, and one allegiance.

The hatred they felt toward the Egyptians prevented intermarriage between the Hebrews and their neighbors. To reap the benefits of the Abrahamic promises, Israel had to remain a pure race, and the Lord used this means to achieve it. They were Semites and white. Yet they lived in the midst of a populace of another hue. To reinforce his purposes in this matter, God prohibited intermarriages.

Keeping their bloodstreams unmixed, becoming a numerous people, and cementing the tribes into a single national body were positively essential to their ultimate destiny.

So it was there in Egypt that the great house of Israel really developed. There it was that the Twelve Tribes were formalized.

But other important factors existed.

Above all else, Israel must accept and preserve the worship of the one and only true God, Jehovah, YHWH! It was Israel, and Israel alone, that was to keep the faith. This could not have been done in Egypt, a land of idolatry, a land of strict monarchical government, a land of magic and wizardry.

Neither would the fires and thunders such as they later experienced on Mt. Sinai have been seen and heard in pagan Egypt. Such were reserved for a time and place when Israel would be alone—by themselves in the wilderness—where God in his majesty could speak to his people without the abrasive influence of magicians and idols. Out there, circumstances would be more conducive to building faith.

The reestablishment of a new line of living prophets was part of the Lord's plan too, and he began it now with his call to Moses. Current and continued revelation would be needed to establish a new way of life for these people who by now had become tolerant of many Egyptian customs.

The worship of Jehovah, YHWH, their Most Holy One, also required temple service that was too sacred to be exposed to the corruptions of pagan Egypt. In God's holy house he would manifest himself to his own, but he would never allow his sanctuary to be built in that land of idols and occult practices. It was to be reserved for that area which he had consecrated in his promise to Abraham. So it must be in Palestine that his chosen priesthood would build his temple in which to perform those holy rites which are so important in the worship of the true God.

Furthermore, the Savior of the world, the great Messiah, was to be born in the Abrahamic lineage. How could this be done except that lineage be preserved in purity? And how could the Savior be born in Bethlehem, the city of David, if Israel did not return to Palestine?

Constituting Israel as a distinct and numerous people in the valleys of the Nile was a great upward step on the ladder of the Almighty. Their stay in that alien land was an obvious segment in their age-long destiny of which even we today are a part.

Yes, Egypt had her role in the Lord's mighty drama, and she played it well.

At the end of 430 years, the Lord now decreed that the time had arrived for Israel to occupy her own land and there become that "peculiar people" who would await the coming of their Messiah.

Chapter 7

THE
PROMISED LAND

What was the Promised Land like in the time of Moses?

The Palestine we know today is arid and for centuries was unproductive and desertlike. The areas now occupied by the Israelis have been made fruitful only by the ambitious irrigation program carried on by that government.

But what was it like when the Lord promised it to Abraham, and when Moses led the Twelve Tribes to the banks of the Jordan?

The scriptures say it was green and beautiful, highly productive, and literally flowing with milk and honey.

However, it was not limited to the narrow strip of land that is modern Palestine. It went far beyond that, extending from the Nile in Egypt to the Euphrates, and was the heartland of the fabled Fertile Crescent, the most productive agricultural portion of that part of the world.

The earliest mention we have of its geographical extent occurs in Genesis where the Lord made his covenant with Abraham: "In the same day the Lord made a covenant with Abram, saying, Unto thy seed have I given this land, from the river of Egypt unto the great river, the river Euphrates." (Genesis 15:18.)

When the Lord mentioned this territory to Moses he used this expression: "And I will set thy bounds from the Red Sea even unto the sea of the Philistines, and from the desert unto the river." (Exodus 23:31.) And when the Lord spoke to Joshua, who was to lead the tribes into the Promised Land, he said: "Every place that the sole of your foot shall tread upon, that have I given unto you, as I said unto Moses. From the wilderness and this Lebanon even unto the great river, the river Euphrates, all the land of the Hittites, and unto the great sea toward the going down of the sun, shall be your coast." (Joshua 1:3-4.)

The Fertile Crescent

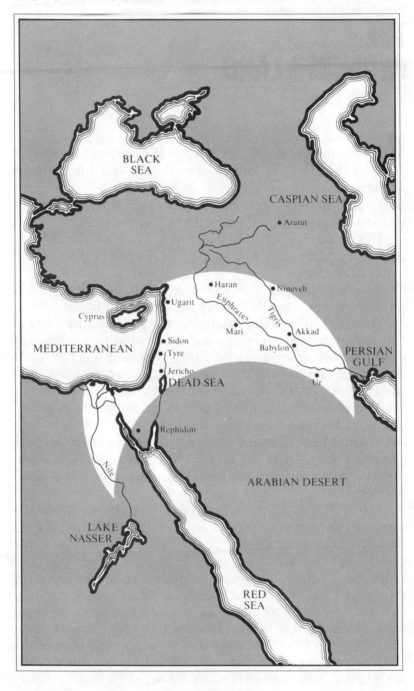

The Land of Promise (Gen. 15:18)

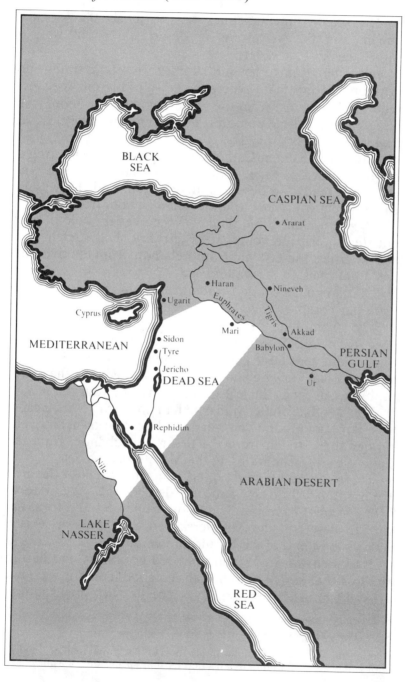

The sea of the Philistines was obviously the Mediterranean, and the wilderness or desert spoken of was, of course, the Arabian desert.

In Deuteronomy eleventh chapter we read a similar description: "Every place whereon the soles of your feet shall tread shall be yours: from the wilderness and Lebanon, from the river, the river Euphrates, even unto the uttermost sea shall your coast be." (V. 24.)

The Knox Roman Catholic Bible gives this rendering of that descriptive passage: "All shall be yours, wherever your feet shall tread; the desert, and Lebanon, and the western sea and the great river Euphrates shall be your frontiers."

The Jerusalem Bible reads: "Wherever the sole of your foot treads shall be yours; your territory shall stretch from the wilderness [desert] and from Lebanon, from the river, the river Euphrates, to the western sea."

That language is almost identical to the modern rendering in the Torah.

The Complete Bible, an American Translation, by Goodspeed and Smith, reads: "Every place on which the sole of your foot treads shall be yours; the region from the desert as far as Lebanon, from the River, the river Euphrates, as far as the Western Sea shall be your domain."

The Moffatt Bible, translated in modern terms, reads: "Every foot of ground you tread shall be your own, and your frontier shall stretch from the desert to Lebânon, from the River, the river Euphrates, to the Mediterranean Sea."

There can be no doubt, then, as to the extent of the area promised to Abraham and his descendants, the Twelve Tribes. It went from the Nile to the Euphrates and from the Arabian desert to the Mediterranean Sea, and was a rich land, the best part of the Fertile Crescent.

How rich was it? Would the Lord give a dry and barren land to Abraham? Would he call it a good land if it were not so? And what about minerals, so necessary to a civilized way of life?

The scripture speaks for itself:

For the Lord thy God bringeth thee into a good land, a land of brooks of water, of fountains and depths that spring out of valleys and hills;

A land of wheat, and barley, and vines, and fig trees, and pomegranates; a land of oil olive, and honey;

A land wherein thou shalt eat bread without scarceness, and thou shalt not lack any thing in it; a land whose stones are iron, and out of whose hills thou mayest dig brass. (Deuteronomy 8:7-9.)

What more could they ask?
The modernized Torah reads:

For the Lord your God is bringing you into a good land, a land with streams and springs and lakes issuing from plain and hill, a land of wheat and barley, of vines, figs, and pomegranates, a land of olive oil and of honey; a land where you may eat food without stint, where you will lack nothing; a land whose rocks are iron and from whose hills you can mine copper. When you have eaten your fill, give thanks to the Lord your God for the good land which He has given you. (Deuteronomy 8:7-10.)

And the Jerusalem Bible reads:

But Yahweh your God is bringing you into a prosperous land, a land of streams and springs, of waters that well up from the deep in valleys and hills, a land of wheat and barley, of vines, of figs, of pomegranates, a land of olives, of oil, of honey, a land where you will eat bread without stint, where you will want nothing, a land where the stones are of iron, where the hills may be quarried for copper. You will eat and have all you want and you will bless Yahweh your God in the rich land he has given you.

Then it was obviously a rich land, rich in water, agriculture, copper, iron, and all else they would need. So when the Lord said it was a good land, he meant just that.

Not even irrigation was needed in Palestine at that time,

for the land, whither thou goest in to possess it, is not as the land of Egypt, from whence ye came out, where thou sowedst thy seed, and wateredst it with thy foot, as a garden of herbs:

But the land, whither ye go to possess it, is a land of hills and valleys, and drinketh water of the rain of heaven:

A land which the Lord thy God careth for: the eyes of the Lord thy God are always upon it, from the beginning of the year even unto the end of the year. (Deuteronomy 11:10-12.)

But what about the milk and honey with which it would flow? Much has been said about the honey, but what of the milk?

When the Israelites scanned the land, "behold the place was a place for cattle." (Numbers 32:1.) And when the scouts sent out by Moses returned and reported to him, they said: "We came unto the land whither thou sentest us, and surely it floweth with milk and honey; and this is the fruit of it," showing him what they had brought. (Numbers 13:27. See also Deuteronomy 1:35; 3:25.)

But as is always the case, the Lord expected the Israelites to be worthy of such a good place in which to live; and he told them frankly that if they failed to keep the commandments, he would withdraw his blessings from the land.

The Canaanites in the land were a wicked and filthy people, and the Lord decreed that they should be swept off the face of this good land, even as were the Sodomites. According to the best references available, they too were sex perverts, and were so disgusting before the Lord that he would no longer allow them to live there. (Deuteronomy 9:4; 12:1-3; Leviticus 18:24.)

He would not destroy them by fire as he did the Sodomites, but he would eliminate them by warfare so that his Twelve Tribes could have the land with a minimum of damage. Says the scripture:

> And it shall be, when the Lord thy God shall have brought thee into the land which he sware unto thy fathers, to Abraham, to Isaac, and to Jacob, to give thee great and goodly cities, which thou buildest not,
> And houses full of all good things, which thou filledst not, and wells digged, which thou diggedst not, vineyards and olive trees, which thou plantedst not; when thou shalt have eaten and be full;
> Then beware lest thou forget the Lord, which brought thee forth out of the land of Egypt, from the house of bondage. (Deuteronomy 6:10-12.)

With this in mind the Lord again warned Israel:

> Hear, O Israel: Thou art to pass over Jordan this day, to go in to possess nations greater and mightier than thyself, cities great and fenced up to heaven,
> A people great and tall, the children of the Anakims, whom thou knowest, and of whom thou hast heard say, Who can stand before the children of Anak!
> Understand therefore this day, that the Lord thy God is he which goeth over before thee; as a consuming fire he shall destroy them, and he shall bring them down before thy face: so shalt thou drive them out, and destroy them quickly, as the Lord hath said unto thee.
> Speak not thou in thine heart, after that the Lord thy God hath cast them out from before thee, saying, For my righteousness the Lord hath brought me in to possess this land: but for the wickedness of these nations the Lord doth drive them out from before thee.
> Not for thy righteousness, or for the uprightness of thine heart, dost thou go to possess their land: but for the wickedness of these nations the Lord thy God doth drive them out from before thee, and that he may perform the word which the Lord sware unto thy fathers, Abraham, Isaac, and Jacob.

Understand therefore, that the Lord thy God giveth thee not this good land to possess it for thy righteousness; for thou art a stiffnecked people. (Deuteronomy 9:1-6.)

How similar were the experiences of these Israelites to those of the Book of Mormon peoples who were blessed abundantly by the Lord while they were humble and righteous, but who forgot the Lord and became worldly when prosperity came to them.

Repeatedly the Nephites were told that if they would obey the God of the land, who was Jesus Christ, they would be prospered in the land, and they were. But also, repeatedly they were told that if they strayed from the truth and allowed their prosperity to blind their eyes to the real facts of life, they would be swept off the land, and they were.

A great lesson regarding human frailty is taught in Helaman 12:1-3 wherein it is shown how quickly even in a very short period of time men turn from righteousness to wickedness. The text reads as follows:

And thus we can behold how false, and also the unsteadiness of the hearts of the children of men; yea, we can see that the Lord in his great infinite goodness doth bless and prosper those who put their trust in him.

Yea, and we may see at the very time when he doth prosper his people, yea, in the increase of their fields, their flocks and their herds, and in gold, and in silver, and in all manner of precious things of every kind and art; sparing their lives, and delivering them out of the hands of their enemies; softening the hearts of their enemies that they should not declare wars against them; yea, and in fine, doing all things for the welfare and happiness of his people; yea, then is the time that they do harden their hearts, and do forget the Lord their God, and do trample under their feet the Holy One—yea, and this because of their ease, and their exceedingly great prosperity.

And thus we see that except the Lord doth chasten his people with many afflictions, yea, except he doth visit them with death and with terror, and with famine and with all manner of pestilence, they will not remember him.

Although many references might be cited in this regard, probably one of the most impressive occurs in 4 Nephi:

And now I, Mormon, would that ye should know that the people had multiplied, insomuch that they were spread upon all the face of the land, and that they had become exceeding rich, because of their prosperity in Christ.

And now, in this two hundred and first year there began to be among them those who were lifted up in pride, such as the wearing of costly apparel, and all manner of fine pearls, and of the fine things of the world.

And from that time forth they did have their goods and their substance no more common among them.

And they began to be divided into classes; and they began to build up churches unto themselves to get gain, and began to deny the true church of Christ.

And it came to pass that when two hundred and ten years had passed away there were many churches in the land; yea, there were many churches which professed to know the Christ, and yet they did deny the more parts of his gospel, insomuch that they did receive all manner of wickedness, and did administer that which was sacred unto him to whom it had been forbidden because of unworthiness.

And this church did multiply exceedingly because of iniquity, and because of the power of Satan who did get hold upon their hearts. (4 Nephi 23-28.)

It is a lesson the Lord has tried to teach his people from the beginning, in both hemispheres. It is a lesson that we of today must yet learn.

Chapter 8

WHO WAS MOSES?

The scripture tells us that Moses was the son of "a man of the house of Levi" who "took to wife a daughter of Levi. And the woman conceived, and bare a son: and when she saw him that he was a goodly child, she hid him three months." (Exodus 2:1-2.)

Then we have the familiar story of the child being left afloat in the river in a basket daubed with slime and pitch:

> And the daughter of Pharaoh came down to wash herself at the river; and her maidens walked along by the river's side; and when she saw the ark among the flags, she sent her maid to fetch it.
> And when she had opened it, she saw the child: and, behold, the babe wept. And she had compassion on him, and said, This is one of the Hebrews' children.
> Then said his sister to Pharaoh's daughter, Shall I go and call to thee a nurse of the Hebrew women, that she may nurse the child for thee?
> And Pharoah's daughter said to her, Go. And the maid went and called the child's mother.
> And Pharoah's daughter said unto her, Take this child away, and nurse it for me, and I will give thee thy wages. And the woman took the child, and nursed it.
> And the child grew, and she brought him unto Pharaoh's daughter, and he became her son. And she called his name Moses: and she said, Because I drew him out of the water. (Exodus 2:5-10.)

In *The Bible Comes Alive,* Sir Charles Marston, British archaeologist, quotes freely from Josephus who writes of Moses' life in Egypt as a young man. The Bible is silent on this portion of his career.

Josephus says that Moses was well educated in Egypt, and this is affirmed by the writer of Acts as he says: "And Moses was learned in all the wisdom of the Egyptians, and was mighty in words and deeds." (Acts 7:22.)

Moses led a military expedition up the Nile and captured Meroe at the junction of the Blue and the White Nile, according to Josephus.

Although they do not mention Moses, the Egyptian records indicate that Queen Hatshepsut sent fleets of ships up the Nile on military expeditions.

Marston says of this queen:

Thus Hatshepsut, because she was Queen Aahmes' daughter, and the descendant of those rulers who had expelled the Hyksos, enjoyed the allegiance of a strong party in Egypt which regarded the blood of her line as alone worthy of royal honours.

Partly on that account, partly because of masterful ability, her father, Thotmes I, associated her with himself in the government about the very time Moses was born. She continued to be the real ruler of Egypt during the reign of Thotmes II, and even for the first sixteen years of Thotmes III, before he became the greatest of the Egyptian conquerors.

Thus, what is known of the biography of this extraordinary woman fits accurately into the Bible references to the daughter of Pharaoh who found the infant Moses floating in the ark of bulrushes on the Nile.

Josephus says her name was Thermuthis. Herein we see an echo of the name Thotmes, which some writers prefer to render as Tahutmes. (*The Bible Comes Alive,* pp. 40-41.)

Marston makes an interesting side comment at this point. He speaks of the antiquity of the moral laws that Moses taught, many of which were already known among the Egyptians of his time. It is another evidence that the gospel, with its moral laws, came down from Adam, even though some became corrupted by the various races that were prominent in antiquity. Marston says:

All this testifies to primeval morality associated with the primeval Monotheism. So the Christian Church did not "invent" the Moral Laws; they were already in existence before Christ. Moses did not make them; they were already in existence before Moses. Archaeology already teaches us that they have come down from the very dawn of civilization. (*The Bible Comes Alive,* p. 43.)

Latter-day Saints know, of course, that this is true, since the gospel was given to Adam and his offspring. It was taught by the prophets both before and after the flood, and was handed on down through the patriarchs Abraham, Isaac, and Jacob, and through Jacob to his descendants.

Marston, the great archaeologist that he is, with all the thoroughness of the typical British scholar, is assured from his studies that Moses was a well-educated man. He points out also that writing and reading were common in Moses' day, and he firmly attacks the critics who say that Moses could not write.

Referring to the writings of the Egyptians, he then says:

> Did it never occur to Bible critics that if Thotmes III could write such records of his life, then Moses must have been able to do the same? And it has now become evident that Moses possessed greater facilities for literary expression than did the Egyptians, although perhaps not so indestructible. (*The Bible Comes Alive,* p. 46.)

Marston also points to the discovery of the Ras Shamra tablets in Syria, as well as to other finds, clearly indicating that there were libraries, schools, and colleges in the period of 1400 to 1350 B.C. Similar discoveries in Babylonia testify to the widespread use of writing in remote ages in that land also.

Then who can say truthfully that Moses was illiterate and unable to write his books of scripture? The facts firmly contradict such criticisms.

Peloubet's *Bible Dictionary* says this regarding Moses' training: "The child was adopted by the princess. From this time for many years Moses must be considered as an Egyptian. As an Egyptian prince he must have a princely education; and he became 'learned in all the wisdom of the Egyptians' (Acts 7:22), who were then unsurpassed in civilization and learning by any people in the world." (F.N. Peloubet, *Bible Dictionary,* Grand Rapids: Zondervan, 1967, p. 421.)

This book also indicates that the name Moses was from the Egyptian *Mes* or *Mesu,* meaning the extraction of a son. Some say it was a Coptic name, meaning saved from the water.

But in spite of all the training that Moses received in Egypt and the debt that he apparently owed to the Pharaoh's daughter, he was still determined to be Hebrew. It is significant that the apostle Paul wrote:

> By faith Moses, when he was come to years, refused to be called the son of Pharaoh's daughter;
> Choosing rather to suffer affliction with the people of God, than to enjoy the pleasures of sin for a season;
> Esteeming the reproach of Christ greater riches than the treasures in Egypt: for he had respect unto the recompence of the reward.

By faith he forsook Egypt, not fearing the wrath of the king: for he endured, as seeing him who is invisible. (Hebrews 11:24-27.)

Although the Bible mentions that Moses killed an Egyptian for "smiting an Hebrew, one of his brethren," no further detail is given. (Exodus 2:11.)

However, the historian Eusebius says that the slaying was the result of a court intrigue in which certain men plotted to assassinate Moses. In the encounter it is said that Moses successfully warded off the attacker and killed him. (Eusebius IX:27.)

In the Midrash Rabbah, the traditional Jewish commentary on the Old Testament, it is asserted that Moses, with his bare fists, killed an Egyptian taskmaster who was in the act of seducing a Hebrew woman. This is confirmed in the Koran.

Certainly there must have been good reason for Moses' act, and most assuredly the Lord would not have called a murderer to the high office of prophet and liberator for his people Israel.

Chapter 9

THE
MYTHICIZED MOSES

There is a true Moses, and there is likewise a mythicized one, made up of the legends of the past and the conjectures of the present. Let us first talk about the legendary Moses.

Says Funk and Wagnall's *Jewish Encyclopedia:*

> Of all Biblical personages, Moses has been chosen most frequently as the subject of later legends, and his life has been recounted in full detail in the poetic Haggadah. As liberator, lawgiver and leader of a people which was transformed by him from an unorganized horde into a nation, he occupies a more important place in popular legend than the Patriarchs and all the other national heroes.
>
> His many sided activity also offered more abundant scope for imaginative embellishment. A cycle of legends has been woven around nearly every trait of his character and every event of his life; and groups of the most different and often contradictory stories have been connected with his career. (Vol. 9, p. 48.)

One of the legends says that Noah was not really worthy to be saved from the flood, but that he was spared because Moses was destined to be one of his descendants.

The angels Jacob saw in his vision at night are alleged to have been Moses and Aaron.

One story says that the birth of Moses as the liberator of his people was foretold to Pharaoh by his soothsayers, which was the reason the king had the Israelite children destroyed.

Another of these yarns says that Moses was born already circumcised, and that as soon as he came into this world he was fully able to walk. When he was born, the story says, a heavenly light filled the home of his parents. He was also able to talk as soon as he was born. When he was three years of age he began to prophesy, the legend goes.

It was said also that when Moses was discovered in the bulrushes, he looked silently into the face of the Egyptian princess. It was necessary for the angel Gabriel to spank the baby to make him cry and thus evoke the sympathy of the princess so that she would adopt him, the tale continues.

Another story says that shortly after Moses was born, the soothsayers identified him to Pharaoh as the liberator of Israel, upon which the king revoked his order to kill all the Israelite babies. One story says that prior to this event, a half million or more Hebrew children had been cast into the river, and that now Moses is regarded as the one who had saved the lives of all who were subsequently born to the Israelites.

It is said that the princess gave Moses his name because she had saved him from the river. But between the Egyptians and the Hebrews, it is said that Moses was given ten names altogether, including Heber, Jared, Gedor, Abi Soko, Jekuthiel, Abi Zanoah, and Shemaiah.

At the age of three, it was told, Moses was a very large and precocious child. One day while sitting at the king's table in the presence of his courtiers, he took the crown off the king's head and put it upon his own head. The princes, of course, were horrified, and immediately the soothsayers predicted that this was the child who would destroy the kingdom of Pharaoh and liberate the Hebrews.

According to the book of Jubilees, he is said to have mastered the writing of the Assyrians.

The legends say that from childhood Moses knew he was a Hebrew, even while in the court of Pharaoh, and he often went out among the enslaved Israelites and showed great sympathy for them. He helped those who were too weak to bear their burdens, and appealed to Pharaoh to have mercy on them.

He is also said to have asked Pharaoh to give the Hebrews one day a week off to rest from their labors, and Pharaoh granted his request. The story claims that this was the origin of the Sabbath Day observance among the Hebrews.

One story says that Moses had many enemies in the court of Pharaoh, some of whom slandered him before the king. This raised enmity between the king and Moses, and eventually Moses had to leave Egypt.

The story relates that he then went to Ethiopia, where he married a Cushite (Ethiopian) woman, and at the age of twenty-seven years he became king of Ethiopia, where he ruled for forty years. Then it was (after these forty years) that his Cushite wife accused him before the princes of refusing to cohabitate with her, and also of refusing to worship the Ethiopian gods.

The princes liked Moses, the legend says, for he had been a good leader; but they also feared the queen. Therefore, they talked the situation over with Moses and persuaded him to leave Ethiopia in peace, which he did.

The legend says it was then that he went to Midian, to the home of Jethro. But Jethro distrusted him and placed him in a deep dungeon, where he was fed only on small portions of bread and water. However, Jethro's daughter Zipporah fell in love with Moses and secretly fed him, thus saving his life.

After ten (or seven) years of this imprisonment, Zipporah reminded her father that he had been keeping Moses in prison this long time; that if he was still alive, he must have survived by some miracle; and that, therefore, he must be a man beloved of God.

The legend says that Jethro then went to the dungeon, found Moses alive and well, and released him. Jethro had in his garden a marvelous rod engraved with the name of God in Hebrew: YHWH. It was said that he asked every man who wanted to marry one of his daughters to attempt to pull this rod out of the ground; none was able to do so until Moses came along, and he did so with little or no effort. Jethro then recognized Moses as the deliverer of Israel and gave him a magic rod. Later, using this rod, he performed the miracles before Pharaoh.

Another legend says that when Moses and Aaron went to see Pharaoh, they met two leopards at the entrance. These animals would never allow anyone to pass unless the guards quieted them. But when Moses approached, they acted like pets, and he played with them as though they were little house cats.

At the time of the exodus, it is said, Moses went to obtain

Joseph's coffin and found it guarded by vicious dogs whose barking could be heard throughout Egypt. But when he came near, the dogs remained still, and he took Joseph's mummy from among the royal tombs without incident.

Many are the legends that have developed around the exodus itself, one of which pertains to the tabernacle. During the seven days of dedication of this portable structure, Moses took it down every night and reassembled it again every morning. One account says that he did this throughout the forty years of the Israelites' travels.

When the seven days of dedication were over, Moses was alleged to have asked the Lord that two offices in Israel might be handed down to his descendants: one was that of king of Israel; the other was that of high priest. The Lord allegedly denied both requests, for the kingship was to go to David through Judah, and the priestly office to Aaron and his sons.

It was rumored that Moses became a very wealthy man. One account says that it came as a dowry given to him by Jethro. Another says it was booty from Pharaoh, seized when the tribes left Egypt. Another story relates that Moses performed a great miracle in his own behalf, and thereby made himself wealthy.

Another story says that he became rich through breaking the tablets containing the words of God, for these tablets were made of sapphires that Moses kept for himself. Another story says that one day God visited Moses in his tent and revealed to the prophet that in the ground under his tent was a pit filled with precious stones.

One of the fables says that Moses' face was always surrounded by a halo of light that he acquired when he first took hold of the tablets of stone while God held them on one side with angels on the other. Still another story says that when Moses wrote the Torah he used a pen with magic ink, and that one day during his work he inadvertently touched his head with the pen, and this created the halo.

Many are the stories about the death of Moses. One says that he died on Adar 7, his own birthday, when he was 120 years old. Another story says that he died as a hero and was fittingly buried. But others say that actually he did not die at all. One legend says that while he was ascending Mount Abarim with Joshua and Eleazar and the elders of the people, suddenly a cloud enveloped him and took him into heaven.

To explain the account of his burial place, which was known only to God, one story says that "God concealed Moses, keeping him for the life in the future world, and no creature knew where he was."

In the Pseudepigrapha (2:409), there is a quotation from the Midrash Tanchuma Debarim, a Hebew apocalypse, that says that when Moses' life was over, he was transformed into "the form of a fiery angel" and ascended "through the seven heavens." This same volume also gives a legend that when Moses arrived in heaven he saw there the heavenly Jerusalem and the holy temple, both of which were to return to earth in the latter days when God had gathered all Israel from the four quarters of the earth. (R.H. Charles, ed., *The Apocrypha and Pseudepigrapha of the Old Testament,* Oxford: Clarendon Press, 1913.)

In this same volume (2:412) under the title "Moses' unique relation to Judaism," we read: "Pre-existence is here ascribed to Moses, but to him uniquely. In Alexandrian Judaism, it was conceived to be the prerogative of mankind generally." This view is found in the Jewish Book of Wisdom and in 2nd Enoch.

Also in this volume is a chapter entitled "The Assumption of Moses," which likewise teaches that Moses was translated and taken into heaven without tasting death. There Moses is said to be discussing his forthcoming passing with his faithful friend and servant Joshua. The text then reads in part:

> And I shall go to sleep with my fathers. Wherefore, Joshua thou (son of) Nun, (be strong and) be of good courage; (for) God hath chosen (thee) to be minister in the same covenant.
> And when Joshua had heard the words of Moses that were so written in his writing all that he had before said, he rent his clothes and cast himself at Moses' feet. And Moses comforted him and wept with him.
> And Joshua answered him and said: "Why dost thou comfort me, (my) lord Moses? And how shall I be comforted in regard to the bitter

word which thou hast spoken which has gone forth from thy mouth, which
is full of tears and lamentation, in that thou departest from this people?
(But now) what place shall receive thee? Or what shall be the sign that
makes (thy) sepulchre? Or who shall dare to move thy body from thence
as that of a mere man from place to place? For all men when they die
have according to their age their sepulchres on earth; but thy sepulchre is
from the rising to the setting sun, and from the south to the confines of the
north: all the world is thy sepulchre.

"My Lord, thou art departing, and who shall feed this people? Or
who is there that shall have compassion on them and who shall be their
guide by the way? Or who shall pray for them, not omitting a single day,
in order that I may lead them into the land of their forefathers? . . ."
(2:423-24.)

The Assumption of Moses is believed to be a composite
of two apocryphal writings, one called the Testament of
Moses and the other the Assumption.

A Greek version of the entire work appeared in the first
century A.D. and was used by Clement of Alexandria,
Origen, and other Greek writers. It was translated into Latin
by the fifth century. A large fragment of one of its early
manuscripts was found in the sixth century in the Ambrosian
Library in Milan. It is believed to have been written originally by some Pharisaic Quietist and was designed as a
protest against the secularization of the Pharisaic party.

No one regards it as scripture.

Chapter 10

THE
TRUE MOSES

The true Moses was one of the mightiest men of God in all time. He certainly needed no mythology to add luster to his name.

He walked and talked with God, received of divine glory while yet in mortality, was called a son of God, and was in the similitude of the Only Begotten.

He saw the mysteries of the heavens and much of creation, and received laws from God beyond any other ancient man of whom we have record.

The most impressive and convincing information we have regarding this great personage is provided in our own Book of Moses in the Pearl of Great Price. It was given by revelation to the Prophet Joseph Smith, which fact is vital and significant. It explodes forever any notion that Moses was mythological in any sense. He lived. He officiated for God. This we know for a fact because the Almighty himself gave us the correct account of his life.

If we will just keep in mind that the Book of Moses was given to Joseph Smith as modern revelation and is not some imperfect history handed down through the ages, it will solve many problems for us.

Moses is also mentioned frequently in the revelations contained in the Doctrine and Covenants, which again lifts any veil of uncertainty that might remain in our minds.

For example, section 84 confirms the life, the identity, and the divine appointment of Moses. It clears away the legendary mist involving his relationship with Jethro, his father-in-law. We are told that indeed Jethro possessed the holy Melchizedek Priesthood and was the individual chosen of the Lord to confer that priesthood upon Moses.

Jethro was a descendant of Midian, a son of Abraham

and Keturah, and certainly was not an Ethiopian as some
have claimed. The priesthood he held had been handed
down through the prophets from Esaias, who received it
under the hand of God himself.

This was a direct line through Gad, Jeremy, Elihu, and
Caleb, and it was Caleb who ordained Jethro, following
which Jethro confirmed it upon Moses. So direct was the ordination both of Jethro and Moses.

The prophet Esaias, we are told, lived in the days of
Abraham and was blessed of him. Abraham received the
priesthood through the lineage of his fathers "even till Noah;
and from Noah till Enoch, through the lineage of their
fathers; and from Enoch to Abel, who was slain by the
conspiracy of his brother."

Abel "received the priesthood by the commandments of
God, by the hand of his father Adam, who was the first
man." This priesthood "continueth in the church of God in
all generations, and is without beginning of days or end of
years." (D&C 84:7-17.)

All of this information concerning the priesthood is of
particular value in a study of Moses, for it gives us the only
line of ordination to him that we have in existence. It tells us
in no uncertain language, and this by modern revelation,
that Moses was in possession of that priesthood by direct
descent through the prophets. He was truly called of God.

Through the Prophet Joseph Smith the Lord tells us that
Moses attempted to bring the children of Israel into the
presence of God through the power of the priesthood, but
they would not obey. (D&C 84:23-25.)

Obviously this effort on the part of the Lord through
Moses was an attempt to bring the full gospel to the people
when they came out of Egypt. But they were so apostate and
so steeped in the traditions of the Egyptians that they would
not listen to him.

That is why the higher priesthood was taken away and
the lesser priesthood left to administer the "schoolmaster"
that the Lord gave to the people as a means of bringing them
back to Christ. This "schoolmaster" was the law of Moses
and the "preparatory gospel." As section 84 explains:

And this greater priesthood administereth the gospel and holdeth the key of the mysteries of the kingdom, even the key of the knowledge of God.

Therefore, in the ordinances thereof, the power of godliness is manifest.

And without the ordinances thereof, and the authority of the priesthood, the power of godliness is not manifest unto men in the flesh;

For without this no man can see the face of God, even the Father, and live.

Now this Moses plainly taught to the children of Israel in the wilderness, and sought diligently to sanctify his people that they might behold the face of God;

But they hardened their hearts and could not endure his presence; therefore, the Lord in his wrath, for his anger was kindled against them, swore that they should not enter into his rest while in the wilderness, which rest is the fulness of his glory.

Therefore, he took Moses out of their midst, and the Holy Priesthood also;

And the lesser priesthood continued, which priesthood holdeth the key of the ministering of angels *and the preparatory gospel;*

Which gospel is the gospel of repentance and of baptism, and the remission of sins, and the law of carnal commandments, which the Lord in his wrath caused to continue with the house of Aaron among the children of Israel until John, whom God raised up, being filled with the Holy Ghost from his mother's womb.

For he was baptized while he was yet in his childhood, and was ordained by the angel of God at the time he was eight days old unto this power, to overthrow the kingdom of the Jews, and to make straight the way of the Lord before the face of his people, to prepare them for the coming of the Lord, in whose hand is given all power. (D&C 84:19-28. Italics added.)

Brigham Young said at one time: "If they had been sanctified and holy, the Children of Israel would not have traveled one year with Moses before they would have received their endowments and the Melchizedek Priesthood." (*Discourses of Brigham Young,* p. 106.)

At another time President Young said: "Moses held the keys and authority above all the rest upon the earth. He holds the keys of the Priesthood of Melchizedek, which is the Priesthood of the Son of God, which holds the keys of all these Priesthoods, dispensing the blessings and privileges of both Priesthoods to the people, as he did in the days of the Children of Israel when he led them out of Egypt." (*Discourses,* p. 143.)

No one reading the writings of Moses in the Pearl of Great Price can fail to be deeply impressed by them. And keep in mind that these writings were given to Joseph Smith by revelation.

When one wonders how Moses could have written all that appears there, it must be remembered that he, like Joseph Smith, wrote by revelation. He had no other way of learning the details of the creation or of the ministry of Enoch who was taken into heaven together with his city, or details in the life of Noah.

We are reminded of the scripture from Peter in this regard: "Prophecy came not in old time by the will of man: but holy men of God spake as they were moved by the Holy Ghost." (2 Peter 1:21.)

And that is the way holy men, or prophets, wrote also.

The writings of Moses make extremely interesting, informative, and faith-promoting reading.

Think of it! Moses saw God face to face "and he talked with him, and the glory of God was upon Moses; therefore Moses could endure his presence." (Moses 1:2.)

The Lord identified himself to Moses as "the Lord God Almighty, and Endless is my name; for I am without beginning of days or end of years; and is not this endless?" (Moses 1:3.)

The Lord discussed his creations with Moses, and revealed them to him:

> And behold, the glory of the Lord was upon Moses, so that Moses stood in the presence of God, and talked with him face to face. And the Lord God said unto Moses: For mine own purpose have I made these things. Here is wisdom and it remaineth in me.
> And by the Word of my power, have I created them, which is mine Only Begotten Son, who is full of grace and truth.
> And worlds without number have I created; and I also created them for mine own purpose; and by the Son I created them, which is mine Only Begotten. (Moses 1:31-33.)

And then the Lord said, after showing Moses the far reaches of the heavens, "But only an account of this earth, and the inhabitants thereof, give I unto you. For behold, there are many worlds that have passed away by the Word of my power. And there are many that now stand, and innumerable are they unto man; but all things are numbered unto me, for they are mine and I know them." (Moses 1:35.)

The record also reads: "And now, behold, this one thing I show unto thee, Moses, my son; for thou art in the world, and now I show it unto thee. And it came to pass that Moses looked, and beheld the world upon which he was created; and Moses beheld the world and the ends thereof, and all the children of men which are, and which were created; of the same he greatly marveled and wondered." (Moses 1:7-8.)

The Lord revealed to Moses, so that he could write it, the conversation the Almighty had with Enoch, in which again the extent of the Lord's creations were shown: "And were it possible that man could number the particles of the earth, yea, millions of earths like this, it would not be a beginning to the number of thy creations; and thy curtains are stretched out still; and yet thou art there, and thy bosom is there; and also thou art just; thou art merciful and kind forever." (Moses 7:30.)

This seems beyond the ability of mortal men to conceive.

Astronomers tell us that never yet, with their most powerful telescopes, have they seen the outer perimeters of space. Always, beyond the reach of their strongest instruments, there is more space and more creation.

The astronomers speak of the heavens that are relatively close to us, and of our Milky Way, and say that we are but a tiny part of it. The Milky Way is actually a great spiral in the heavens, containing, so the astronomers say, 100 billion suns like ours, plus all their satellites.

This spiral is part of a larger organization containing nineteen such spirals, with other billions upon billions of suns and planets. One astronomer said that if we wish to understand how vast space is, we may know that this larger body, made up of nineteen spirals like and including our Milky Way, is merely tucked away in one corner of the heavens.

Moses knew of this, because he wrote about it, including that which was made known to Enoch as well as that which was made known to him by direct observation while in the presence of God.

We mention this to call attention only to one phase of Moses' life. He knew astronomy and saw the heavens—not from some instrument made by man, but by the power of God.

Moses knew by what power he saw all these things, for he said: "But now mine own eyes have beheld God; but not my natural, but my spiritual eyes, for my natural eyes could not have beheld; for I should have withered and died in his presence; but his glory was upon me; and I beheld his face, for I was transfigured before him." (Moses 1:11.)

It should be plainly evident that Moses was no ordinary man, with ordinary skills or education. He was taught by the Lord himself. Adam had this same experience. Both were highly intelligent; both were educated as few men have been.

When the critics in their ignorance try to downgrade Moses and say that he was incapable of doing the things that the Bible says he did, we realize more than ever that the wisdom of man is as foolishness to God, and we can readily see why.

Moses' encounter with Satan—personally—is a most fascinating part of his writings. All should read it in the first chapter of the Book of Moses in the Pearl of Great Price.

He saw the devil himself. The devil tried to deceive him and presented himself as though he were the Savior. But Moses, inspired as he was, caught the devil in his lie, and by the power of God cast him out of his presence.

The creation story is given in his book in much greater detail than it is in the Bible, but it corroborates the Bible story fully and lets us know that Genesis is a correct though concise story of creation.

Our brief glimpse into the preexistent life, where Jesus was chosen as the Savior, is provided in Moses' writings. The conflict leading up to the war in heaven and the rebellion of Lucifer is explained.

The noble words of God must always be remembered as he speaks of Jehovah's voluntary sacrifice to save mankind:

And I, the Lord God, spake unto Moses, saying: That Satan, whom thou hast commanded in the name of mine Only Begotten is the same which was from the beginning, and he came before me, saying—Behold, here am I, send me, I will be thy son, and I will redeem all mankind, that one soul shall not be lost, and surely I will do it; wherefore give me thine honor.

But, behold, my Beloved Son, which was my Beloved and Chosen from the beginning, said unto me—Father, thy will be done, and the glory be thine forever.

Wherefore, because that Satan rebelled against me, and sought to destroy the agency of man, which I, the Lord God, had given him, and also, that I should give unto him mine own power; by the power of mine Only Begotten, I caused that he should be cast down;

And he became Satan, yea, even the devil, the father of all lies, to deceive and to blind men, and to lead them captive at his will, even as many as would not hearken unto my voice. (Moses 4:1-4.)

The account of the creation of Adam and Eve as the first human beings on the earth is here affirmed. Likewise, the story of the Garden of Eden, the temptation, the fall, and the expulsion into the world as we now know it. All of this is told through the writings of Moses, as revealed and confirmed in modern times by the Lord to Joseph Smith. (Moses 3, 4, and 5.)

The pact made between Cain and Satan is explained, including the murder of Abel. Moses also tells of the conversation between the Lord and Cain following the crime, and the development of the cult of the Master Mahan, in which the great secret was administered unto Cain by Satan.

Was he not a great historian? Did he not write under the dictation of the Holy Spirit, so that he would know these details, even the words of conversations of that early period? These facts were all made known to Moses by revelation, and to us through the writings of that great man.

The story of Enoch and his city and the revelation to Enoch concerning the coming of Christ are set forth:

And it came to pass that Enoch looked; and from Noah, he beheld all the families of the earth; and he cried unto the Lord, saying: When shall the day of the Lord come? When shall the blood of the Righteous be shed, that all they that mourn may be sanctified and have eternal life?

And the Lord said: It shall be in the meridian of time, in the days of wickedness and vengeance.

And behold, Enoch saw the day of the coming of the Son of Man, even in the flesh; and his soul rejoiced, saying: The Righteous is lifted up, and the Lamb is slain from the foundation of the world; and through faith I am in the bosom of the Father, and behold, Zion is with me. (Moses 7:45-47.)

Enoch saw the crucifixion in vision, and Moses described
it in his book:

And the Lord said: Blessed is he through whose seed Messiah shall
come; for he saith—I am Messiah, the King of Zion, the Rock of Heaven,
which is broad as eternity; whoso cometh in at the gate and climbeth up
by me shall never fall; wherefore, blessed are they of whom I have
spoken, for they shall come forth with songs of everlasting joy.

And it came to pass that Enoch cried unto the Lord, saying: When
the Son of Man cometh in the flesh, shall the earth rest? I pray thee, show
me these things.

And the Lord said unto Enoch: Look, and he looked and beheld the
Son of Man lifted up on the cross, after the manner of men;

And he heard a loud voice; and the heavens were veiled; and all the
creations of God mourned; and the earth groaned; and the rocks were
rent; and the saints arose, and were crowned at the right hand of the Son
of Man, with crowns of glory;

And as many of the spirits as were in prison came forth, and stood on
the right hand of God; and the remainder were reserved in chains of darkness until the judgment of the great day. (Moses 7:53-57.)

Some scholars question the flood. By revelation to
Moses, and likewise to Joseph Smith, we know the truth
about the flood:

And Noah was four hundred and fifty years old, and begat Japheth;
and forty-two years afterward he begat Shem of her who was the mother
of Japheth, and when he was five hundred years old he begat Ham.

And Noah and his sons hearkened unto the Lord, and gave heed, and
they were called the sons of God.

And when these men began to multiply on the face of the earth, and
daughters were born unto them, the sons of men saw that those daughters
were fair, and they took them wives, even as they chose.

And the Lord said unto Noah: The daughters of thy sons have sold
themselves; for behold mine anger is kindled against the sons of men, for
they will not hearken to my voice.

And it came to pass that Noah prophesied, and taught the things of
God, even as it was in the beginning.

And the Lord said unto Noah: My Spirit shall not always strive with
man, for he shall know that all flesh shall die; yet his days shall be an
hundred and twenty years; and if men do not repent, I will send in the
floods upon them.

And in those days there were giants on the earth, and they sought
Noah to take away his life; but the Lord was with Noah, and the power of
the Lord was upon him.

And the Lord ordained Noah after his own order, and commanded
him that he should go forth and declare his Gospel unto the children of
men, even as it was given unto Enoch.

And it came to pass that Noah called upon the children of men that
they should repent; but they hearkened not unto his words;

And also, after that they had heard him, they came up before him, saying: Behold, we are the sons of God; have we not taken unto ourselves the daughters of men? And are we not eating and drinking, and marrying and giving in marriage? And our wives bear unto us children, and the same are mighty men, which are like unto men of old, men of great renown. And they hearkened not unto the words of Noah.

And God saw that the wickedness of men had become great in the earth; and every man was lifted up in the imagination of the thoughts of his heart, being only evil continually.

And it came to pass that Noah continued his preaching unto the people, saying: Hearken, and give heed unto my words;

Believe and repent of your sins and be baptized in the name of Jesus Christ, the Son of God, even as our fathers, and ye shall receive the Holy Ghost, that ye may have all things made manifest; and if ye do not this, the floods will come in upon you; nevertheless they hearkened not.

And it repented Noah, and his heart was pained that the Lord had made man on the earth, and it grieved him at the heart.

And the Lord said: I will destroy man whom I have created, from the face of the earth, both man and beast, and the creeping things, and the fowls of the air; for it repenteth Noah that I have created them, and that I have made them; and he hath called upon me; for they have sought his life.

And thus Noah found grace in the eyes of the Lord; for Noah was a just man, and perfect in his generation; and he walked with God, as did also his three sons, Shem, Ham, and Japheth.

The earth was corrupt before God, and it was filled with violence.

And God looked upon the earth, and, behold, it was corrupt, for all flesh had corrupted its way upon the earth.

And God said unto Noah: The end of all flesh is come before me, for the earth is filled with violence, and behold I will destroy all flesh from off the earth. (Moses 8: 12-30.)

Then came the flood.

What a bulwark to our faith is Moses! How close he lived to the Lord in order to receive his many blessings!

How can anyone, having the actual facts, doubt that Moses was truly one of the elect of God, a mighty prophet, the deliverer of his people?

Chapter 11

MOSES AND PHARAOH

The conflict of opposing forces was never more clearly defined than in the confrontation of Moses and Pharaoh.

To begin with, Moses was frightened to appear in the Egyptian royal court. There were probably many reasons. Of course he was the meekest of all men (Numbers 12:3) and depreciated his own abilities.

Moses evidently also had recollections of his earlier departure from Egypt, when he was forced to flee because of his fight with the Egyptian taskmaster.

Pharaoh must have recognized Moses, who grew to manhood in the royal courts, a protege of the princess who had found him in the bulrushes. But God had a work for Moses to do, and would take no excuses. He must "set my people free."

The angel of the Lord appeared to Moses in a flame of fire out of the midst of a bush, and he turned to see this phenomenon.

And when the Lord saw that he turned aside to see, God called unto him out of the midst of the bush, and said, Moses, Moses. And he said, Here am I.

And he said, Draw not nigh hither: put off thy shoes from off thy feet, for the place whereon thou standest is holy ground.

Moreover he said, I am the God of thy father, the God of Abraham, the God of Isaac, and the God of Jacob. And Moses hid his face; for he was afraid to look upon God.

And the Lord said, I have surely seen the affliction of my people which are in Egypt, and have heard their cry by reason of their taskmasters; for I know their sorrows;

And I am come down to deliver them out of the hand of the Egyptians, and to bring them up out of that land unto a good land and a large, unto a land flowing with milk and honey. . . .

Now therefore, behold, the cry of the children of Israel is come unto me: and I have also seen the oppression wherewith the Egyptians oppress them.

Come now therefore, and I will send thee unto Pharaoh, that thou mayest bring forth my people the children of Israel out of Egypt. (Exodus 3:4-10.)

As he did subsequently, so Moses now questioned the Lord, asking, "Who am I, that I should go unto Pharaoh, and that I should bring forth the children of Israel out of Egypt?" (Exodus 3:11.)

The story of his interview with the Lord is well known, as is the call of Aaron to assist him. But before they could confront Pharaoh they must win over the elders of Israel.

And Moses and Aaron went and gathered together all the elders of the children of Israel:

And Aaron spake all the words which the Lord had spoken unto Moses, and did the signs in the sight of the people.

And the people believed: and when they heard that the Lord had visited the children of Israel, and that he had looked upon their affliction, then they bowed their heads and worshipped. (Exodus 4:29-31.)

Any fear that Moses had of being trapped by his former enemies was removed when the Lord told him that "all the men are dead which sought thy life." (Exodus 4:19.)

So now the time came for Moses and Aaron to face Pharaoh. There is a lack of agreement among various scholars as to which of the Egyptian kings this was. Some believe that Rameses II was the pharaoh of the liberation, while others believe that he was the king who enslaved Israel. These latter scholars claim that the pharaoh of the deliverance was actually Merneptah II, who was the thirteenth son of Rameses II.

Regardless of identification, the pharaoh of the enslavement was determined to subdue the Hebrews, as was also the pharaoh of the liberation.

The Egyptians were builders and needed slave labor. They also had but shortly before that time driven the foreign Hyksos usurpers from the throne and from the country, and they feared yet another invasion. Since the Hebrews lived in an area of the Delta that would provide easy access for any invader, the Egyptians were fearful that they might join some invasion force to obtain their own liberty.

These important elements figured prominently in the confrontation between Moses and Pharaoh. Neither Pharaoh

nor Moses would yield. It was a situation almost like the irresistible force meeting the immovable object.

The *New Analytical Bible* says:

To realize in any proper sense the nature and significance of these
events we must take our stand in the Egypt of that day and watch this
mighty contest.

On the one side is the greatest state of antiquity of that time having a
highly developed civilization. It was this nation that lit the torch of civilization and passed it on to the West. They were a deeply religious people
having a system that was replete with deities. They had their priests and
magicians.

On the other side was a despised and enslaved nation, two men,
Moses and Aaron, and the God of Israel. What a spectacle as these two
men, armed with nothing more than a shepherd's crook, stand before the
mighty Pharaoh, and in the name of Jehovah demand that he permit the
people to leave the land!

When he refused, a new thing happened that transcended the natural
and human.

The Nile was an Egyptian deity and it was smitten by a Power greater
than Egypt's god and the latter was discredited. What a shock it must have
been to the Egyptian mind that his great god [the river] was so completely
subjected to the Will of a greater being whom these two messengers call
Jehovah and in whose name they speak and act.

The very significant thing about these plagues is the fact that they
demonstrate the presence and power of a Being above Nature and superior to the gods upon whom Egypt relied.

The fish of the Nile, one of the staple commodities of food, died.
Their god [the Nile] could not save itself or the life it contained. Ra, the
Sun-god, was their chief object of worship, but was powerless to give them
light during the three days of midnight darkness, while in Goshen it was
light.

Beasts were the representatives of some of their deities, particularly
the bull, and they were destroyed by a murrain.

Thus were the plagues designed to expose to Pharaoh and his people
the utter folly of their idolatry and to open their eyes to the true God.
When the plague of lice spread over the land they declared this to be "the
finger of God."

With what force it must have come to Pharaoh when he ascertained
that in Goshen where dwelt the enslaved Hebrews there were no murrain,
no darkness, no hail, no locusts and finally no destruction of their
firstborn.

How profoundly and completely did the God of Israel vindicate
Himself in this land steeped in the most abominable idolatry. (Chicago:
John A. Dickson Publishing Co., 1947, p. 119.)

Moses was as persistent as Pharaoh was stubborn. The
scripture repeatedly tells how Pharaoh hardened his heart
against Moses and the prophet's proposals. Instead of yielding in any degree, Pharaoh increased the burdens of the Hebrew slaves, and this too added to Moses' discomfort when

the Israelites railed against him for it. They took the position that instead of Moses bringing about their liberation, he was only making their bondage worse.

Pharaoh cried out insultingly against Moses and said, "Who is the Lord, that I should obey his voice to let Israel go? I know not the Lord, neither will I let Israel go." (Exodus 5:2.)

And when Moses and Aaron told the king that they had met with their God, who again had commanded them to liberate Israel, the king merely replied: "Get you unto your burdens."

It was then that the straw was taken from the Hebrews as they made bricks, and "let there more work be laid upon the men, that they may labor therein; and let them not regard vain words."

Now Moses complained to the Lord. "Wherefore hast thou so evil entreated this people? . . . For since I came to Pharaoh to speak in thy name, he hath done evil to this people; neither hast thou delivered thy people at all." (Exodus 5:2, 4, 9, 22-23.)

These were hard words that Moses spoke to the Lord. But God knew what he was about. There was purpose in all he did, and as he permitted Pharaoh to resist, he also was teaching the monarch that the God of Israel was mightier than the gods of Egypt. This lesson was not alone for the Egyptians, either, for the Israelites themselves had to learn that great fact, inasmuch as many of them had become worshipers of the Egyptian deities.

The Lord was under covenant to bring his people out, and he would keep his word, so he said to Moses:

Wherefore say unto the children of Israel, I am the Lord, and I will bring you out from under the burdens of the Egyptians, and I will rid you out of their bondage, and I will redeem you with a stretched out arm, and with great judgments:

And I will take you to me for a people, and I will be to you a God: and ye shall know that I am the Lord your God, which bringeth you out from under the burdens of the Egyptians.

And I will bring you in unto the land, concerning the which I did swear to give it to Abraham, to Isaac, and to Jacob; and I will give it you for an heritage: I am the Lord. (Exodus 6:6-8.)

But when Moses carried that message to the people,

"they hearkened not unto Moses for anguish of spirit, and for cruel bondage." (Exodus 6:9.)

Between the complaints of the people and the resistance of the king, Moses had a difficult time. The Lord was now ready to perform miracles, however, to harass the Egyptians into submission. Some were defiantly duplicated by the magicians. But then the plagues came. The Nile was turned to blood. The fish died. There was an invasion of frogs. Pharaoh prayed for deliverance from them. The plague of lice followed, making Pharaoh more bitter and stubborn.

The flies and murrain were next, but although the Egyptians suffered, the Israelites in the land of Goshen were free from it all. Next came the boils, which affected even the magicians, regardless of their magic.

Hail and locusts now afflicted Egypt, but none were found in Goshen. At last the king began to relent. But it wasn't enough, so darkness came upon the land except in Goshen, where there was light. Pharaoh weakened a little more, but even yet he refused to free the slaves.

And then came the final blow—the death of the firstborn of all life in Egypt, again excepting the Israelites, who were saved by the Passover.

Not only did Pharaoh permit the Israelites to leave; he commanded them to go. The Egyptian people themselves hurried the Israelites in their departure, fearing that even they themselves would die, as had their firstborn children.

And it came to pass, when Pharaoh had let the people go, that God led them not through the way of the land of the Philistines, although that was near; for God said, Lest peradventure the people repent when they see war, and they return to Egypt:

But God led the people about, through the way of the wilderness of the Red sea: and the children of Israel went up harnessed out of the land of Egypt.

And Moses took the bones of Joseph with him: for he had straitly sworn the children of Israel, saying, God will surely visit you; and ye shall carry up my bones away hence with you.

And they took their journey from Succoth, and encamped in Etham, in the edge of the wilderness.

And the Lord went before them by day in a pillar of a cloud, to lead them the way; and by night in a pillar of fire, to give them light; to go by day and night:

He took not away the pillar of the cloud by day, nor the pillar of fire by night, from before the people. (Exodus 13:17-22.)

Chapter 12

THE PLAGUES WERE MIRACLES

Critics of the Bible have unmercifully attacked the account of the plagues used by the Lord to persuade Pharaoh to release the Hebrew slaves. Some say the story of the plagues is but another part of Bible mythology. Others try to explain them by natural means—"if they really happened at all."

There is this constant refusal on the part of these scholars to accept anything that is miraculous, because, of course, they are not even sure that there is a God in heaven at all, and if there is none, how could there be miracles? Hence they either discard these accounts altogether or try to explain them as natural phenomena and not without precedent.

Then there are some scholars who are willing to go half way in their acceptance of the miraculous, but who still cling to their reservations. Such a one is this:

The ten plagues which facilitated the departure of the Israelites were—with the exception of the last, the slaughter of the first-born of Egypt—natural phenomena of Egypt, and the miracle of them is that they were either intensified or that they occurred at unusual times. With the tenth plague it may be that, in fact, only the first-born of the Pharaoh died. (*The Bible Companion,* p. 11.)

With regard to this Sir Charles Marston, British archaeologist and defender of the Bible, has written:

The Ten Plagues of Egypt followed the refusal of Pharaoh. These carry us again into the sphere of the so-called supernatural or miraculous. On the other hand, they may be described as a succession of misfortunes that befell the Egyptians, most of which at any rate may be attributed to natural causes.

It has been the custom in the past for those who disbelieved in miracles to explain the Ten Plagues on these lines. Now that so-called miracles are being recognized by Science, it is no longer necessary to overemphasize natural causes. In doing so, while we are rescuing unusual events from one form of miracle in order to satisfy superficial knowledge, yet on the other hand, we are really consigning them into a region of more profound mystery.

What is the nature of natural causes? Why do things happen as they do, and when they do?

The Bible, as the text-book of the Science of Man, teaches us that the Deity works through natural causes. And again, according to scripture, Nature itself and its Laws *are God's handiwork,* and He is Immanent in them.

Too much emphasis has perhaps been laid upon the uniformity of Nature. The weather, for example, is not uniform, life is not uniform, even matter itself seems to be no longer regarded as entirely uniform.

In considering the cause of such incidents as the Plagues of Egypt, it is well to bear in mind that calamities are not uniform. When we come to incidents associated with the crossing of Jordan by the Israelites under Joshua, and the fall of the walls of Jericho, it will be seen that earthquakes were the immediate cause of them.

The fact that these incidents, like the Ten Plagues of Egypt, *happened when they did,* constitute the real miracle and point to the Ultimate Cause. For the rest, the Plagues of Egypt for the most part have occurred in Egypt at other times, except perhaps the last and greatest, the death of the firstborn, including the death of Pharaoh's eldest son. (*The Bible Comes Alive,* p. 47. Italics added.)

Stephen L. Caiger, in his book *Bible and Spade,* mentions a monument in Egypt that seems to confirm the account of the unexpected death of Pharaoh's son. (Quoted in Marston, *The Bible Comes Alive,* p. 48.)

When new translations of the Bible have been undertaken, a most careful search has been made for all manuscript sources, and some of the finest scholars in the translation field have been assigned to the work. In many instances the scholarship of these translators far exceeds that of the Bible critics who make their derogatory comments largely out of personal opinion only.

The new translations of the Bible completely and in detail confirm the King James version of the entire drama of the liberation. This includes what is said concerning the plagues that preceded the deliverance, and shows that they were indeed miraculous, both in their timing and in their effectiveness.

Note a few verses from the Jerusalem Bible, one of the finest of the new versions on the market today.

Concerning the water turning to blood we read:

Yahweh the God of the Hebrews has sent me (Moses) to say (to Pharaoh): Let my people go to offer me worship in the wilderness. Now, so far you have not listened. Here is Yahweh's message: That I am

Yahweh. You shall learn by this: with the staff that is in my hand I will strike the water of the river and it shall be changed into blood. The fish in the river will die, and the river will smell so foul that the Egyptians will not want to drink the water of it. (Exodus 7:16-18.)

Some of the critics who insist that all was natural phenomena claim that sediment that had been washed into the river from heavy rains upstream gave a reddish color to the water. Do they recall how little it rains in that part of the world? And would sediment in the river cause a stench?

The literalness of the description of what followed, as given in the Jerusalem Bible, shows the futility of any such argument. Says the text:

Moses and Aaron did as Yahweh commanded. He raised his staff in the sight of Pharaoh and his court [it is interesting that it was done in the presence of the royal party], he struck the waters of the river and all the water in the river changed to blood. . . . Meanwhile all the Egyptians dug holes along the banks of the river in search of drinking water; they found the water of the river impossible to drink. (Exodus 7:20-25.)

The new version of the Torah issued by the Jewish Publication Society of America, Philadelphia, reads as follows on this point:

"Let My people go that they may worship Me in the wilderness." But you have paid no heed until now. Thus says the Lord, "By this you shall know that I am the Lord." See, I shall strike the water in the Nile with the rod that is in my hand, and it will turn into blood; and the fish in the Nile will die. The Nile will stink so that the Egyptians will find it impossible to drink the water of the Nile.

And the Lord said to Moses, "Say to Aaron: Take your rod and hold out your arm over the waters of Egypt—its rivers, its canals, its ponds, all its bodies of water—that they turn to blood; there shall be blood throughout the land of Egypt, even in vessels of wood and stone."

Moses and Aaron did just as the Lord commanded: he lifted up the rod and struck the water in the Nile in the sight of Pharaoh and his courtiers, and all the water in the Nile was turned into blood and the fish in the Nile died. The Nile stank so that the Egyptians could not drink water from the Nile; and there was blood throughout the land of Egypt. . . . And all the Egyptians had to dig round about the Nile for drinking water because they could not drink the water of the Nile. (Torah, Exodus 7:16-24.)

Could this have happened from sediment washed downstream? Moses restored the water to normal at the Lord's discretion, which was another miracle.

When the flies came, Moses specified to Pharaoh the

exact time they would go away, "and Yahweh did as Moses asked; the gadflies left Pharaoh and his courtiers and his subjects; not one remained." (Jerusalem Version, Exodus 8:31-32.)

When the plague of murrain came upon the cattle, "the Egyptian livestock died, but none owned by the sons of Israel died. Pharaoh had inquiries made, but it was true; none was dead of the livestock owned by the sons of Israel. But Pharaoh became adamant again and did not let the people go." (Ibid., 9:7.)

When it came to the final plague, when the firstborn of all Egypt was taken, human and animal life were included, not just the son of Pharaoh, as some claim. Says the Jerusalem Version: "At midnight Yahweh struck down all the first-born in the land of Egypt; the first-born of Pharaoh, heir to his throne, the first-born of the prisoner in his dungeon, and the first-born of all the cattle." (Ibid., 12:29.)

The revised Torah says: "There was no house where there was not someone dead." (Exodus 12:30.)

The other new versions agree with these. The plagues were deliberate; they were timed carefully; they had definite reactions from Pharaoh. They were brought upon Egypt as Pharaoh looked on so that he knew what was going on. He was a personal witness to it all. He knew they were miracles. He knew that it was Jehovah in action. Knowing this full well, he said to Moses: "Entreat Yahweh to rid me and my subjects of the frogs, and I promise to let the people go." (Jerusalem Version, Exodus 8:1-10.)

When the three days of darkness came, we read in the Jerusalem Version: "Then Yahweh said to Moses, 'Stretch out your hand towards heaven and let darkness, darkness so thick that it can be felt, cover the land of Egypt.' So Moses stretched out his hand towards heaven, and for three days there was deep darkness over the whole land of Egypt. No one could see anyone else or move about for three days, but where the sons of Israel lived there was light for them." (Ibid., 10:21-23.)

The critics try to explain this period of darkness as an

eclipse. But does an eclipse last for three days? Does it cover only selected parts of an area?

This darkness is reminiscent of that which came to America during the crucifixion. Of that situation the Book of Mormon says:

> And it came to pass that when the thunderings, and the lightnings, and the storm, and the tempest, and the quakings of the earth did cease—for behold, they did last for about the space of three hours; and it was said by some that the time was greater; nevertheless, all these great and terrible things were done in about the space of three hours—and then behold, there was darkness upon the face of the land.
>
> And it came to pass that there was thick darkness upon all the face of the land, insomuch that the inhabitants thereof who had not fallen could feel the vapor of darkness;
>
> And there could be no light, because of the darkness, neither candles, neither torches; neither could there be fire kindled with their fine and exceedingly dry wood, so that there could not be any light at all;
>
> And there was not any light seen, neither fire, nor glimmer, neither the sun, nor the moon, nor the stars, for so great were the mists of darkness which were upon the face of the land.
>
> And it came to pass that it did last for the space of three days that there was no light seen; and there was great mourning and howling and weeping among all the people continually; yea, great were the groanings of the people, because of the darkness and the great destruction which had come upon them. (3 Nephi 8:19-23.)

Our modern scriptures are positive in declaring that the Lord did bring Israel out of the land of Egypt (1 Nephi 17:40) and with a mighty hand. In other words, he did it miraculously.

Although the Israelites did "harden their hearts from time to time, and they did revile against Moses, and also against God; nevertheless, ye know that they were led forth by his matchless power into the land of promise." (1 Nephi 17:42.)

Nephi comments further as to the miraculous events of the exodus as he says:

> And he did straiten them in the wilderness with his rod; for they hardened their hearts, even as ye have; and the Lord straitened them because of their iniquity. He sent fiery flying serpents among them; and after they were bitten he prepared a way that they might be healed; and the labor which they had to perform was to look; and because of the simpleness of the way, or the easiness of it, there were many who perished. (1 Nephi 17:41.)

When Joseph in Egypt spoke of a seer to be raised up in the latter days, he said: "And he shall be great like unto Moses, whom I have said I would raise up unto you, to deliver my people, O house of Israel. And Moses will I raise up, to deliver thy people out of the land of Egypt." (2 Nephi 3:9-10.)

The fact that God *delivered* Israel by the hand of Moses itself implies the miraculous.

There is similar corroboration in this:

And now, my brethren, I have spoken plainly that ye cannot err. And as the Lord God liveth that brought Israel up out of the land of Egypt, and gave unto Moses power that he should heal the nations after they had been bitten by the poisonous serpents, if they would cast their eyes unto the serpent which he did raise up before them, and also gave him power that he should smite the rock and the water should come forth; yea, behold I say unto you, that as these things are true, and as the Lord God liveth, there is none other name given under heaven save it be this Jesus Christ, of which I have spoken, whereby man can be saved. (2 Nephi 25:20.)

And still further support is given in Alma as we read:

And I know that he will raise me up at the last day, to dwell with him in glory; yea, and I will praise him forever, for he has brought our fathers out of Egypt, and he has swallowed up the Egyptians in the Red Sea; and he led them by his power into the promised land; yea, and he has delivered them out of bondage and captivity from time to time. (Alma 36:28.)

The Book of Mormon peoples obtained information concerning the exodus from the brass plates of Laban. They contained "engravings, which have the records of the holy scriptures upon them," and therefore we do not question them. (Alma 37:1-12.)

Dr. J. O. Kinnaman, writing in *Digger for Facts,* says this:

The climax of the whole situation was the death of the firstborn of man and beast. At this point, the adverse critics for a long time thought that they had discredited the Bible archaeologist; but God still works in a wondrous way to vindicate His Word.

From archaeological evidence [inscriptions] we know that Merneptah [who is believed to have succeeded Ramses II] was not succeeded on the throne by his oldest son. We are told that this boy died suddenly and unexpectedly while still very young. This death occurred about the time recorded in the Bible as the time of the death of the firstborn. *This event took place according to the best chronology April 6-7 (midnight).* (Massachusetts: Destiny Publishers, 1940, p. 103. Italics added.)

We who are interested in the date of April 6 will be pleased to note what this archaeologist says about the time of the final decision of Pharaoh to "let my people go."

April 6. Very interesting indeed!

There is wide disparity among the scholars as to the year of the exodus. The suppositions range anywhere from 1230 to 1491 B.C. Most, however, believe it took place about 1290 B.C.

Chapter 13

THE PASSOVER

The Almighty brought Israel out of Egypt through a series of wondrous miracles. The entire procedure was without either parallel or precedent.

As the people traveled in the daytime, the Lord led the way. At night they were guided by a luminous cloud. They were given safe passage through the Red Sea, and they saw Pharaoh's pursuing armies swallowed up in the deep. They were fed for forty years in the desert as only the Almighty could provide for such a multitude. Their clothes never wore out.

They watched Moses ascend the heights of Sinai to commune with the Lord; they saw him return with a heavenly glow upon his face, and they were awed. They saw the lightning and heard the thunder as the Lord descended upon the mount, personally announcing the Ten Commandments, and they were frightened, fearing for their lives.

The entire drama of the exodus was a constant display of heavenly compassion, determination, at times indignation, and mighty power. It is no wonder that the Israelites have been impressed by it as by few other events in their history.

But with it all, the most significant event was the introduction of the Passover.

Nothing in their entire experience so partook of the divine nature as did this great event. Nothing else was intended quite so much to teach them the meaning of their relationship to God. The paschal lamb of that day could only refer to the Lamb of God. It was a divine symbol.

As we look back upon it now, we can readily see that the Passover truly was a pattern of Christ's great sacrifice. The Israelites, however, did not seem to understand it at the time. They were too involved in the mechanics of their escape. But

Moses, who wrote of Christ, must have known that the Passover was symbolic of the Savior's sacrifice on the cross. Certainly Paul in a later dispensation knew very well indeed, for he wrote that *Christ is our passover.*

In writing to the Corinthians, persuading them to truly worship the Lord, he said: "Purge out therefore the old leaven, that ye may be a new lump, as ye are unleavened. For even *Christ our passover* is sacrificed for us: Therefore let us keep the feast, not with old leaven, neither with the leaven of malice and wickedness; but with the unleavened bread of sincerity and truth." (1 Corinthians 5:7-8.)

How many times is the Savior called the Lamb of God?

John the Baptist, standing with his followers, pointed to Jesus and said, "Behold the Lamb of God." (John 1:29.)

Peter spoke of him as the Paschal Lamb when he said, "Ye were not redeemed with corruptible things, as silver and gold, from your vain conversation received by tradition from your fathers; *But with the precious blood of Christ as of a lamb without blemish and without spot:* Who verily was fore-ordained before the foundation of the world." (1 Peter 1:18-20. Italics added.)

Jesus of Nazareth was indeed the Lamb of God.

Did not John the Revelator in his vision see ten thousand times ten thousand say with a loud voice: "Worthy is the Lamb that was slain to receive power, and riches, and wisdom, and strength, and honour, and glory, and blessing. And every creature which is in heaven, and on the earth, and under the earth, and such as are in the sea, and all that are in them, heard I saying, Blessing, and honour, and glory, and power, be unto him that sitteth upon the throne, and unto the Lamb for ever and ever." (Revelation 5:11-13.)

When Joseph Smith and Sidney Rigdon looked into the heavens they saw "the holy angels, and them who are sanctified before his throne, worshiping God, and the Lamb, who worship him forever and ever." (D&C 76:21.)

They also saw the ultimate glory and triumph of the Lamb "who was slain, who was in the bosom of the Father before the worlds were made." (D&C 76:39.)

As they closed their account of this magnificent revelation, they wrote: "And to God and the Lamb be glory, and honor, and dominion forever and ever." (D&C 76:119.)

Those who say that the plague of the death of the firstborn in Egypt was an isolated natural incident or that it did not happen at all must find some explanation for the powerful and meaningful symbolism in that event. God has often taught in symbols. He has often instructed his children by showing them "types of things to come." This last plague was too symbolic and too important as a prophetic type of things to come to have been but a human invention.

Christ was the Father's Firstborn. He was the Lamb of God. The Passover was in every way symbolic of his great sacrifice.

As the Lord gave instruction to Moses concerning the paschal lamb on that first Passover, he required that the lamb must be a male without blemish of any kind. The Savior, in his sacrifice, was without blemish.

In the first paschal lamb, no bone was to be broken. In the Savior's crucifixion, no bone was broken. (Exodus 12:5, 46; John 19:36.)

The blood of the paschal lamb of Moses' day was the means by which the ancient Israelites were spared from the angel of death.

To all of us the blood of the Christ is our means of escaping the devil, who is the worst of all the angels of death and destruction. By serving the Lord, his blood rescues us—saves us—from Satan, and helps us to return to the presence of our Heavenly Father.

As the blood of the first paschal lamb meant life, not death, to ancient Israel, so is the blood of Christ to all mankind a symbol, assuring us of life, not death, eternally.

Christ is our Paschal Lamb. His passover is forever, if we will accept it, not just for a single night as it was in Egypt. It should be far more meaningful to us than was escape from the angel of death to the Hebrews.

The offering of sacrifices to the Lord began with Adam. These burnt offerings were symbolic of the coming atonement of the Christ. They continued from Adam to the days of John the Baptist. The ultimate sacrifice of the Savior on

Calvary brought an end to such sacrifices and introduced the sacrament of the Lord's Supper in their place.

The burnt offerings of ancient times looked forward to the coming sacrifice of the Lamb of God; the sacrament of the Lord's Supper looks back to that sacrifice, and therefore we eat and drink of the sacred emblems in remembrance of him. Our sacramental prayers explain the sacred nature of that ordinance.

The paschal lamb of Egypt was, of course, a sacrifice, but with a greatly enlarged significance. Instead of the blood of the sacrifice being disposed of in the usual way, this time the blood was to be placed upon the door posts *as a sign* to the destroying angel that here lived believers. The presence of that blood would spare all their firstborn from death. It literally symbolized life and salvation for Israel in the face of death and destruction for the Egyptians.

Throughout the centuries since then, the Passover has been observed by the Jews as one of their most important holy anniversaries.

Jesus himself observed it. When he was found in the temple as a boy of twelve, his presence in Jerusalem was in observance of the Passover. (Luke 2:41-42.) As he became a man, he likewise honored that day. It was most significant to him, since he himself was the great Paschal Lamb.

As he came to Jerusalem for the last time, his disciples asked him, "Where wilt thou that we prepare for thee to eat the passover?" (Matthew 26:17.)

He said, "Go into the city to such a man, and say unto him, The Master saith, My time is at hand; I will keep the passover at thy house with my disciples." The disciples "did as Jesus had appointed them; and they made ready the passover." (Matthew 26:18-19.)

This was the most important of all passovers, that to which all previous ones looked forward. It was the time of the great sacrifice, the atonement of the Lord.

He sat down to supper with the Twelve, and—

As they did eat, he said, Verily I say unto you, that one of you shall betray me.

And they were exceeding sorrowful, and began every one of them to say unto him, Lord, is it I?

And he answered and said, He that dippeth his hand with me in the dish, the same shall betray me.

The Son of man goeth as it is written of him: but woe unto that man by whom the Son of man is betrayed! it had been good for that man if he had not been born.

Then Judas, which betrayed him, answered and said, Master, is it I? He said unto him, Thou hast said. (Matthew 26:21-25.)

Now was the time all burnt offerings should end. Now, as he was about to be sacrificed himself, he changed the ordinance and introduced the sacrament of the Lord's Supper:

And as they were eating, Jesus took bread, and blessed it, and brake it, and gave it to the disciples, and said, Take, eat; this is my body.

And he took the cup, and gave thanks, and gave it to them, saying, Drink ye all of it;

For this is my blood of the new testament, which is shed for many for the remission of sins.

But I say unto you, I will not drink henceforth of this fruit of the vine, until that day when I drink it new with you in my Father's kingdom.

And when they had sung an hymn, they went out into the mount of Olives.

Then saith Jesus unto them, All ye shall be offended because of me this night: for it is written, I will smite the shepherd, and the sheep of the flock shall be scattered abroad.

But after I am risen again, I will go before you into Galilee. (Matthew 26:26-32.)

Then came the touching scene where Peter was rebuked: "This night, before the cock crow, thou shalt deny me thrice."

And now came the prayer and suffering in Gethsemane. The Lamb indeed was to be sacrificed. He was to take upon himself the suffering of all mankind.

Then cometh Jesus with them unto a place called Gethsemane, and saith unto the disciples, Sit ye here, while I go and pray yonder.

And he took with him Peter and the two sons of Zebedee, and began to be sorrowful and very heavy.

Then saith he unto them, My soul is exceeding sorrowful, even unto death: tarry ye here, and watch with me.

And he went a little further, and fell on his face, and prayed, saying, O my Father, if it be possible, let this cup pass from me: nevertheless not as I will, but as thou wilt.

And he cometh unto the disciples, and findeth them asleep, and saith unto Peter, What, could ye not watch with me one hour?

Watch and pray, that ye enter not into temptation: the spirit indeed is willing, but the flesh is weak.

He went away again the second time, and prayed, saying, O my

Father, if this cup may not pass away from me, except I drink it, thy will be done.

And he came and found them asleep again: for their eyes were heavy.

And he left them, and went away again, and prayed the third time, saying the same words.

Then cometh he to his disciples, and saith unto them, Sleep on now, and take your rest: behold, the hour is at hand, and the Son of man is betrayed into the hands of sinners.

Rise, let us be going: behold, he is at hand that doth betray me. (Matthew 26:36-46.)

On the Passover night in Egypt there was no betrayal. On this, the Great Passover, there was the following:

And while he yet spake, lo, Judas, one of the twelve, came, and with him a great multitude with swords and staves, from the chief priests and elders of the people.

Now he that betrayed him gave them a sign, saying, Whomsoever I shall kiss, that same is he: hold him fast.

And forthwith he came to Jesus, and said, Hail, master; and kissed him.

And Jesus said unto him, Friend, wherefore art thou come? Then came they, and laid hands on Jesus, and took him.

And, behold, one of them which were with Jesus stretched out his hand, and drew his sword, and struck a servant of the high priest's, and smote off his ear.

Then said Jesus unto him, Put up again thy sword into his place: for all they that take the sword shall perish with the sword.

Thinkest thou that I cannot now pray to my Father, and he shall presently give me more than twelve legions of angels?

But how then shall the scriptures be fulfilled, that thus it must be?

In that same hour said Jesus to the multitudes, Are ye come out as against a thief with swords and staves for to take me? I sat daily with you teaching in the temple, and ye laid no hold on me.

But all this was done, that the scriptures of the prophets might be fulfilled. Then all the disciples forsook him, and fled. (Matthew 26:47-56.)

The account of the crucifixion is well known. It was indeed the enactment of the Great Passover. The Lamb of God was now offered up, the Lamb "slain from the beginning of the world," the Lamb of God!

This gives added meaning to our faith as we look back at the Passover of Moses' day. Without the offering of the Lamb of God on Calvary, there would be no salvation, "for there is none other name under heaven given among men, whereby we must be saved." (Acts 4:12.)

The Jews, even today, still observe the Passover as instituted in Moses' day. In Hebrew the word is *Pesach,* meaning to pass over or to spare. As *The Book of Jewish Knowledge* describes it:

"The most beloved of all Jewish holy days is the festival of Passover. Symbolically, in its most meaningful sense, it represents a cherished traditional Jewish value—a love of freedom. That is the reason why, in the religious literature of the Jews, the festival is referred to pridefully as 'The Season of Our Freedom.' " (New York: Crown Publishers, 1964, p. 324.)

This volume, produced by Nathan Ausubel, goes on to explain that elaborate preparations are made for the festival, which lasts eight days now, although prior to the Middle Ages the duration was for only seven days.

In every home a search is made for even the smallest crumb of leavened bread, which must be banished from the house, for only matzah, unleavened bread, may be eaten at this time.

A number of symbolic foods are required, such as the shankbone of a roasted lamb, called *z'roah;* a *beitzah,* roasted egg, and bitter herbs to remind the Jews of the bitterness of the Egyptian bondage. Other significant foods are also used, and all are put on a "Passover plate" for serving. Reading the Haggadah narrative about the bondage and liberation in Egypt is an important part of the observance.

The celebration is now largely a family affair, and although the liberation is remembered solemnly, the Jews make a major point of emphasizing family love and unity and adherence to the faith of their fathers.

Much as the Passover is Jewish, Christians must recognize in it a symbol of the atonement of Christ, for it was definitely such.

Dr. James E. Talmage gives a touching description of the Lord's suffering in Gethsemane:

Christ's agony in the garden is unfathomable by the finite mind, both as to intensity and cause. The thought that He suffered through fear of death is untenable. Death to Him was preliminary to resurrection and triumphal return to the Father from whom He had come, and to a state of glory even beyond what He had before possessed; and, moreover, it was within His power to lay down His life voluntarily.

He struggled and groaned under a burden such as no other being who has lived on earth might even conceive as possible. It was not physical pain, nor mental anguish alone, that caused Him to suffer such torture as to produce an extrusion of blood from every pore; but a spiritual agony of soul such as only God was capable of experiencing.

No other man, however great his powers of physical or mental endurance, could have suffered so; for his human organism would have succumbed, and syncope would have produced unconsciousness and welcome oblivion.

In that hour of anguish Christ met and overcame all the horrors that Satan, "the prince of this world" could inflict. The frightful struggle incident to the temptations immediately following the Lord's baptism was surpassed and overshadowed by this supreme contest with the powers of evil.

In some manner, actual and terribly real though to man incomprehensible, the Savior took upon Himself the burden of the sins of mankind from Adam to the end of the world. Modern revelation assists us to a partial understanding of the awful experience.

In March 1830, the glorified Lord, Jesus Christ, thus spake: "For behold, I, God, have suffered these things for all, that they might not suffer if they would repent, but if they would not repent, they must suffer even as I, which suffering caused myself, even God, the greatest of all, to tremble because of pain, and to bleed at every pore, and to suffer both body and spirit: and would that I might not drink the bitter cup and shrink—nevertheless, glory be to the Father, and I partook and finished my preparations unto the children of men."

From the terrible conflict in Gethsemane, Christ emerged a victor. Though in the dark tribulation of that fearful hour He had pleaded that the bitter cup be removed from His lips, the request, however oft repeated, was always conditional; the accomplishment of the Father's will was never lost sight of as the object of the Son's supreme desire.

The further tragedy of the night, and the cruel inflictions that awaited Him on the morrow, to culminate in the frightful tortures of the cross, could not exceed the bitter anguish through which He had successfully passed. (*Jesus the Christ,* pp. 613-14.)

The Savior's own description of his suffering is probably the most poignant expression we have in all our literature:

Therefore I command you to repent—repent, lest I smite you by the rod of my mouth, and by my wrath, and by my anger, and your sufferings be sore—how sore you know not, how exquisite you know not, yea, how hard to bear you know not.

For behold, I, God, have suffered these things for all, that they might not suffer if they would repent;

But if they would not repent they must suffer even as I;

Which suffering caused myself, even God, the greatest of all, to tremble because of pain, and to bleed at every pore, and to suffer both body and spirit—and would that I might not drink the bitter cup, and shrink—

Nevertheless, glory be to the Father, and I partook and finished my preparations unto the children of men.

Wherefore, I command you again to repent, lest I humble you with my almighty power; and that you confess your sins, lest you suffer these punishments of which I have spoken, of which in the smallest, yea, even in the least degree you have tasted at the time I withdrew my Spirit. (D&C 19:15-20.)

Chapter 14

THE EXODUS FROM EGYPT

Who can measure the magnitude of the exodus of Israel from the land of the Nile? That journey is beyond the comprehension of modern people accustomed to present-day conveniences and equipment. There is nothing known in history to compare with it.

When we think of the travels of our own pioneers from Nauvoo to the Great Basin, we are appalled at their hardships and accomplishments. But they were numbered only in the thousands, and their trek was spaced over twenty-two years. From the first company led by Brigham Young in 1847 to the coming of the railroad in 1869, a total of some 80,000 pioneers migrated to Utah.

They came in separate contingents and many were well equipped. We had our handcart pioneers, of course, all of whom walked across the plains, a number of them dying on the way. And many of those who drove ox teams also walked. With their wagons reserved to carry their heavy loads, members of families, including little children, trudged on foot the entire distance from the Missouri River to the Great Salt Lake. Their hardships were almost beyond belief.

But consider the situation faced by Moses and his people in their exodus. Once the plagues had convinced Pharaoh that he must free the Israelites, it seemed that the Egyptians could hardly wait to see the last of them, for they now feared for their own lives.

> And it came to pass, that at midnight the Lord smote all the firstborn in the land of Egypt, from the firstborn of Pharaoh that sat on his throne unto the firstborn of the captive that was in the dungeon; and all the firstborn of cattle.
>
> And Pharaoh rose up in the night, he, and all his servants, and all the Egyptians; and there was a great cry in Egypt; for there was not a house where there was not one dead.

And he called for Moses and Aaron by night, and said, Rise up, and get you forth from among my people, both ye and the children of Israel; and go, serve the Lord, as ye have said.

Also take your flocks and your herds, as ye have said, and be gone; and bless me also.

And the Egyptians were urgent upon the people, that they might send them out of the land in haste; for they said, We be all dead men. (Exodus 12:29-33.)

Their haste in leaving was such that "the people took their dough before it was leavened, their kneadingtroughs being bound up in their clothes upon their shoulders," and left. This was their fresh dough intended for baked bread. So great was their haste.

The modernized Torah records the situation as follows:

And Pharaoh arose in the night, with all his courtiers and all the Egyptians—because there was a loud cry in Egypt; for there was no house where there was not someone dead.

He summoned Moses and Aaron in the night and said, "Up, depart from among my people, you and the Israelites with you! Go, worship the Lord as you said! Take also your flocks and your herds as you said, and be gone!"

The Torah also explains that the "Egyptians urged the people on, to make them leave in haste, for they said, 'We shall all be dead.' So the people took their dough before it was leavened, their kneading bowls wrapped in their cloaks upon their shoulders." (Torah, Exodus 12:30-34.)

There can be no doubt that the flight was in haste. But consider the extent of it.

The scripture says there were 600,000 men and their families. If we were to estimate 600,000 men plus 600,000 women plus their numerous children (for the record says they were very prolific), there must have been at least two or three million people who hastily took what they could carry and left. By comparison, it may be remembered that the total population of Utah today is only a little more than one million, and that the present population of modern Israel in Palestine is only about three million.

The scripture refers to the total body of Israelites as being likened to the "stars of heaven for multitude." (Deuteronomy 10:22.) A similar expression occurs in

Deuteronomy 1:10. At one time they had a standing army of 400,000 foot soldiers. (Judges 20:2, 17.)

When a plague struck the camp and 14,700 died, it did not seem to make any discernible dent in the total number. (Numbers 16:49.)

When a subsequent census was taken of persons over twenty, "these were numbered of the children of Israel 601,730." (Numbers 26:4, 51.)

It seems difficult to determine with any accuracy the total number of the Twelve Tribes at the time of the exodus, but indeed they were a numerous host.

The people and animals all went in a single large company, as far as can be determined from the record. Think of driving many thousands of animals before them, to say nothing of the families caring for themselves. Think of the pregnant women, and the little children, and recall how the Savior, foretelling the destruction of Jerusalem, urged the people to pray that their flight be not in haste, for he knew the extent of the problem.

Some idea of the number of their animals may be obtained from reading Numbers 31:42-46, where mention is made of 337,500 sheep and 36,000 head of cattle.

Many westerners in the United States have had experience herding cattle and sheep from one grazing area to another, and they know the difficulties involved. Animals travel slowly and they wander. They need grazing, and they need water. The Israelites had all these problems. Moses had been a herdsman himself, but at no time did he seem to have more than a small herd of sheep, and they belonged to Jethro.

Let us admit that what Moses achieved was beyond all human capabilities. The Lord was with him, and it was the Lord's doing. As the scripture teaches, nothing is too hard for the Lord. (Genesis 18:14.) Such a trek as this could not possibly have been made without constant divine assistance and direction. But such help was given. It was a tremendous miracle.

We have some excellent examples of how the Lord

performs this type of miracle, as we read in the Book of Mormon.

The people of Limhi, in escaping from the Lamanites, "did depart by night into the wilderness with their flocks and their herds," and the fast-moving armies of the Lamanites tried for two days to catch up with them but could not. Consider that for a moment. The people of Limhi traveled with their flocks and herds, but even the fleet-footed Lamanite armies could not catch them, and they had only a short headstart. (Mosiah 22:10-16.)

How was it done? It is further illustrated in the escape of Alma's people from the armies of King Noah: "They gathered together their flocks, and took of their grain, and departed into the wilderness before the armies of King Noah. *And the Lord did strengthen them,* that the people of King Noah could not overtake them to destroy them. And they fled eight days' journey into the wilderness." (Mosiah 23:1-3. Italics added.) It was another miracle.

The Lord strengthened Alma's people further while they were captives of King Amulon so that although as slaves they were laden with heavy burdens the Lord blessed them to the point where "you cannot feel them upon your backs, even while you are in bondage." (Mosiah 24:14-15.)

The Bible Companion, a rather critical volume, considering its name, questions the exodus account but does admit that the Jews believed and accepted the story all down through the ages. Says this volume: "Legend invariably attaches itself to great events, and the supreme figures in a nation's history have their exploits magnified. With Moses, it is impossible that he should have been, or done, all that the biblical tradition credits him with."

This is the tone of most critics who are unwilling to grant anything miraculous in the Bible. Then it goes on:

But that he [Moses] was an actual person, and that he led his people from slavery, and mediated the covenant at Sinai which became their national and religious heritage, few scholars today deny.

There can be no doubt that the Israelites themselves regarded that complex of events made up of the deliverance from Egypt, the crossing of the Red Sea, the making of the covenant, the giving of the Law at Mount Sinai, and the wanderings in the wilderness, as the great constitutive factor of their history, the great beginning, which they never stopped remembering and to which they always looked back. In every strand of the Old Testament the wonder and the might of it is remembered. Prophets recall it, and so do psalmists, and preachers as well. (*The Bible Companion,* p. 11.)

That volume also discounts the other miracles of Moses. It even indicates that Pharaoh's son was the only one killed on the night of the Passover. But that, of course, is only poor conjecture on the part of some speculative scholars.

According to the best estimates, the total population of Egypt, not counting the Israelites, was about eleven million people at the time of the exodus. But again, there are no firm census figures available.

Frequent mention is made in the scriptures of the prolific nature of the Hebrews. This was one of the main reasons Pharaoh enslaved them. He was fearful that they might join some enemy army in taking over the government. This, of course, gives further meaning to the following: "And the children of Israel were fruitful, and increased abundantly, and multiplied, and waxed exceeding mighty; and the land was filled with them." (Exodus 1:7.)

Funk and Wagnall's *Jewish Encyclopedia* (5:294) reviews the biblical data, but then joins the uninspired critics and says:

That the events narrated in Exodus cannot be historical in all their details has been generally conceded. The numbers are certainly fanciful: 600,000 men would represent a total of at least two million souls. Where these could have found room and subsistence in the land of Goshen, granted even that many of them lived in Pharaoh's capital, or in the district of Rameses, and how so vast an unorganized host could have crossed the Red Sea in one night are questions that have not been explained. The exodus must have been a movement of a much smaller body of men.

That again is only poor conjecture by skeptics. All we actually have by way of facts on the subject is from the scripture itself, and the various new translations as well as the Torah and "The Holy Scriptures" according to the Masoretic text, sustain the King James Version. As has been noted, archaeology is making the scripture less and less subject to challenge.

The Jerusalem Bible, a strictly modern version, bearing

the imprimatur of the Roman Catholic Church, has this to say:

> And at midnight Yahweh struck down all the first-born in the land of Egypt; the first-born of Pharaoh, heir to his throne, the first-born of the prisoner in his dungeon, and the first-born of all the cattle.
>
> Pharaoh and all his courtiers and all the Egyptians got up in the night, and there was a great cry in Egypt, for there was not a house without its dead.
>
> And it was night when Pharaoh summoned Moses and Aaron. "Get up," he said, "you and the sons of Israel, and get away from my people. Go and offer worship to Yahweh as you have asked, and, as you have asked, take your flocks and herds, and go. And also ask a blessing on me."
>
> The Egyptians urged the people to hurry up and leave the land, because, they said, "Otherwise we shall all be dead." So the people carried off their dough, still unleavened, on their shoulders, their kneading bowls wrapped in their cloaks. (Jerusalem Version, Exodus 12:29-34.)

This Bible is the work of both French and British scholars and was translated from the ancient texts. It is the English equivalent of the French *La Bible de Jerusalem*. (Doubleday, 1966.)

The Moffatt Bible gives this interesting statement: "The Egyptians pressed the people to hurry out of the land, crying, 'We are all dead men!' "

But all of these Bibles, and others not quoted here, hold to the 600,000 men, plus the families, as the number who escaped. Whether we wish to question those figures in the ancient manuscripts and believe the speculations of the skeptics is something each one must decide for himself.

One of the Jewish legends about the birth of Moses and the slaying of the boy babies says that Pharaoh had half a million of the Hebrew children destroyed before he ended the slaughter. If there is any shadow of truth in that story, it would suggest a population of several million to have so many babies. The fact is that revelation confirms many of the details of the exodus, although modern scripture says nothing about the total number who left.

There are a few indications of Israel's size, however, as seen from some of the census figures provided in the Bible.

The sons of Levi are listed, and likewise the children of these sons. For example, the male members of the family of Gershon, son of Levi, are listed at 7,500, not counting any girls or women. Of the children of Kohath, there were 8,600 males. Of the family of Merari, there were 6,200 men and boys.

Then we have this scripture: "All that were numbered of the Levites, which Moses and Aaron numbered at the commandment of the Lord, throughout their families, all the males from a month old and upward, were twenty and two thousand." (See Numbers 3:1-39.) This, of course, relates only to the tribe of Levi.

The scripture then follows with a count of all firstborn males in all the tribes of Israel, with no others but the firstborn included:

> And the Lord said unto Moses, Number all the firstborn of the males of the children of Israel from a month old and upward, and take the number of their names.
> And thou shalt take the Levites for me (I am the Lord) instead of all the firstborn among the children of Israel; and the cattle of the Levites instead of all the firstlings among the cattle of the children of Israel.
> And Moses numbered, as the Lord commanded him, all the firstborn among the children of Israel.
> And all the firstborn males by the number of names, from a month old and upward, of those that were numbered of them, were twenty and two thousand two hundred and threescore and thirteen. (Numbers 3:40-43.)

Of course there is no way of estimating the total population merely from the number of firstborn men and boys, since there is no record of the other members of the families.

As Joshua began his wars against the sinful inhabitants of the land, he "chose out thirty thousand mighty men of valour" to attack the enemy. (Joshua 8:3.)

To raise an army of 30,000 "mighty men of valour" would indicate he had a large population to draw from. But again, it is not known whether this was his total army or merely a contingent chosen for a special military task. In the battle 12,000 of the enemy "fell that day." (Joshua 8:25.)

The book of Ezra gives an interesting sidelight on the movement of large bodies of people. When the Jews returned from their Babylonian captivity, it was recorded as follows:

> The whole congregation together was forty and two thousand three hundred and threescore,

Beside their servants and their maids, of whom there were seven thousand three hundred thirty and seven: and there were among them two hundred singing men and singing women.

Their horses were seven hundred thirty and six; their mules, two hundred forty and five;

Their camels, four hundred thirty and five; their asses, six thousand seven hundred and twenty. (Ezra 2:64-67.)

So we might go on. But we must remember that all the objections of the critics are conjectural. Attacks on various phases of Holy Writ have come to failure as archaeology and other research have unearthed facts that sustain the Bible.

Of course the task of removing the Israelites from Egypt under conditions of such haste was beyond human effort. But if the Lord was able to divide the Red Sea, if he could feed the hosts and provide water for them in a desert where neither of these life-giving elements was naturally available, he certainly could have—and did—otherwise expedite their flight.

If the Lord was able to transport the whole city of Enoch into heaven, would he not be able to expedite the movement of the Israelites out of Egypt?

Let us not forget that the Book of Mormon authenticates "the five books of Moses," and surely the author of those five books knew what he was talking about. (1 Nephi 5:11.)

Concerning the exodus, *The Bible Companion* (p. 163) says:

Tradition is emphatic that *this was no mere escape story, nor the work of Moses. Moses was but the human instrument in a mighty act of deliverance wrought by Yahweh.* . . .

From this moment, Israel's religion can claim to be firmly rooted, not in speculation about the nature of the Infinite, but in a series of historical events in which Yahweh takes the initiative to deliver his people. (Italics added.)

The Book of Mormon, on which we can wholly depend, is certainly not silent with respect to the exodus. The dividing of the waters of the Red Sea is mentioned repeatedly, so there certainly is no myth about that.

For example, Nephi, speaking to his brethren as they were seeking the plates of Laban, said: "Therefore let us go up; let us be strong like unto Moses; for he truly spake unto the waters of the Red Sea and they divided hither and thither, and our fathers came through, out of captivity, on dry ground, and the armies of Pharaoh did follow and were drowned in the waters of the Red Sea." (1 Nephi 4:2.)

This, to us, is revelation—from God—in these modern times, and completely destroys the position of the critics who say that Israel did not pass through the Red Sea, that the Red Sea was not even involved in the escape, and that Pharaoh's army was not destroyed in the sea.

Later in his first book, Nephi again affirms the escape of the Twelve Tribes from Egyptian bondage and declares that it was by the hand of God that it was all accomplished. Then he says:

"Now ye know that Moses was commanded of the Lord to do that great work; and ye know that by his word the waters of the Red Sea were divided hither and thither, and they passed through on dry ground. But ye know that the Egyptians were drowned in the Red Sea, who were the armies of Pharaoh."

He also confirms the account of manna being provided by the Lord for the Israelites, for he says: "And ye also know that they were fed with manna in the wilderness."

Then he authenticates the account of Moses striking the rock when there was no water in the desert: "Yea, and ye also know that Moses, by his word according to the power of God which was in him, smote the rock, and there came forth water, that the children of Israel might quench their thirst." (1 Nephi 17:22-29.)

Again, this comes to us by modern revelation through the translation and publication of the Book of Mormon. There is no room to doubt the account since it is thus confirmed. Again we see the value of the two sticks that Ezekiel saw (Ezekiel 37), both in our hand today, each one confirming the other.

In the book of Helaman also, we have proof of the Red Sea crossing. A later Nephite prophet spoke: "Behold, my brethren, have ye not read that *God gave power unto one man, even Moses,* to smite upon the waters of the Red Sea, and they parted hither and thither, insomuch that the Israelites, who were our fathers, came through upon dry ground, and the waters closed upon the armies of the Egyptians and swallowed them up?" (Helaman 8:11. Italics added.)

Why should any Latter-day Saint doubt the story of the Red Sea crossing with this kind of corroboration? The Book of Mormon is true! It is God's word to us of today!

When the Lord talked with Moses, as is recorded in the first chapter of Moses in the Pearl of Great Price, the Lord predicted that the waters would be subject to Moses. He said: "And calling upon the name of God, he beheld his glory again, for it was upon him; and he heard a voice, saying: Blessed art thou, Moses, for I, the Almighty, have chosen thee, and thou shalt be made stronger than many waters; for they shall obey thy command as if thou wert God." (Moses 1:25.)

But not only do the Book of Mormon and the Pearl of Great Price give proof of the fact of the Red Sea crossing— so also does the Doctrine and Covenants.

The Lord, speaking to Oliver Cowdery, said: "Now, behold, this is the spirit of revelation; behold, this is the spirit by which Moses brought the children of Israel through the Red Sea on dry ground." (D&C 8:3.)

The Red Sea crossing is therefore established beyond any doubt whatever. On the word of the Lord himself, this event took place.

The miracle was repeated as the Israelites crossed over the Jordan and into the Promised Land. They went dry shod over the streambed, and when they were on the other side, the waters returned to their usual place. (See Joshua 3:15-17; 4:7; 4:18; 5:1.)

When there are doubts about the colossal nature of the undertaking, let us remember that the Book of Mormon also confirms the presence of God in that exodus, and proves that it was by his almighty power that the undertaking was accomplished, since it was far beyond human limitations. And what uninspired scholars can understand the miracles of God?

Again let us refer to Nephi: "And notwithstanding they being led, the Lord their God, their Redeemer, going before them, leading them by day and giving light unto them by night, *and doing all things for them which were expedient for man to receive,* they hardened their hearts and blinded their minds, and reviled against Moses and against the true and living God." (1 Nephi 17:30. Italics added.)

Here is language that no Latter-day Saint can ignore, coming as it does from the Book of Mormon.

Note that it was Jesus Christ, our Redeemer, our Lord and God, who went before them and guided them both by night and by day. It was the Savior, the Creator of all the worlds, who opened the Red Sea, which swallowed up the armies of Pharaoh; who brought forth water in the desert when Moses struck the rock; who provided the manna and the quail; and who did all other miracles so necessary to the movement of such a large body of people and their possessions.

Let us ask by way of comparison:

Since Christ, being Jehovah and Creator, brought into existence all of the universes in the heavens, including our own little earth and its oceans, was he not quite able to divide the Red Sea, which was but one of his very minor creations?

Since the Savior, as Creator, had made all the heavenly bodies and put adequate water on this earth, which is but a mere speck in space, was he not able to create a refreshing spring in the desert?

And since he is the Master of life and death, and soon was to vanquish death by his own resurrection, was he not qualified to stave off death by starvation on behalf of his wandering people?

Is anything too hard for the Lord?

He is Almighty God!

The exodus was a miraculous event!

Let us accept it as such and not try to explain it away by human means. We have revelation, and revelation is far more to be desired than the speculations of uninspired minds, no matter how well educated in worldly things they may be.

The Lord had pledged to Abraham half a millennium

before that he would give the Holy Land to Israel as a home, and that meant moving Israel out of Egypt. But his people were enslaved there. They were victims of a cruel monarchical regime. They were powerless to chart their own course. Being in bondage, they literally were unable to act for themselves. Therefore the Almighty moved on their behalf.

It is admitted that the exodus was beyond the mortal powers of Moses, and the prophet himself knew that. He was even afraid to face Pharaoh, knowing his own limitations. He also feared the elders of Israel, thinking that they would not accept him as one sent of God. Moses knew his own shortcomings well enough to realize that the exodus was far beyond his power to accomplish.

But with God, nothing is impossible, and it was the Lord who now undertook the task, using Moses as his humble instrument.

How many times does Holy Writ declare that it was God who brought Israel out of Egypt! It is evident throughout the scriptures. Yes, it was he who did it, and by that same power which called all creation into being in the first place.

Chapter 15

MOSES AND THE PRIESTHOOD

The gospel of the Lord Jesus Christ was taught to Adam and his family and to the patriarchs down to Moses' day. The object of that dispensation of gospel truths was the same as it is today: to bring the children of God back into his presence.

Moses made a great effort to teach the Twelve Tribes those simple truths. Salvation came anciently as it does now, through the ministration of the priesthood, "which priesthood continueth in the church of God in all generations, and is without beginning of days or end of years," as the Lord says in the Doctrine and Covenants. (D&C 84:17.)

Moses received the Holy Priesthood under the hands of his father-in-law Jethro, and Jethro received it through the fathers back to the days of Abraham and Melchizedek. (D&C 84:6-14.)

The revelation then continues:

And the Lord confirmed a priesthood also upon Aaron and his seed, throughout all their generations, which priesthood also continueth and abideth forever with the priesthood which is after the holiest order of God.

And this greater priesthood administereth the gospel and holdeth the key of the mysteries of the kingdom, even the key of the knowledge of God.

Therefore, in the ordinances thereof, the power of godliness is manifest.

And without the ordinances thereof, and the authority of the priesthood, the power of godliness is not manifest unto men in the flesh;

For without this no man can see the face of God, even the Father, and live.

Now this Moses plainly taught to the children of Israel in the wilderness, and sought diligently to sanctify his people that they might behold the face of God;

But they hardened their hearts and could not endure his presence; therefore, the Lord in his wrath, for his anger was kindled against them, swore that they should not enter into his rest while in the wilderness, which rest is the fulness of his glory.

Therefore, he took Moses out of their midst, and the Holy Priesthood also;

And the lesser priesthood continued, which priesthood holdeth the key of the ministering of angels *and the preparatory gospel;*

Which gospel is the gospel of repentance and of baptism, and the remission of sins, *and the law of carnal commandments,* which the Lord in his wrath caused to continue with the house of Aaron among the children of Israel until John, whom God raised up, being filled with the Holy Ghost from his mother's womb. (D&C 84:18-27. Italics added.)

Moses obviously endeavored to have his people accept the gospel of Christ, which could bring them back into the divine presence. But when they rejected the gospel, and when Moses and the higher priesthood were taken away, they were left only with the Aaronic Priesthood and the lesser ordinances.

The Lord also gave to Israel in the wilderness a book of "Doctrine and Covenants" (Ex. 24:7, 8) which is found in Exodus 20:22 to 23:33. This was accepted by the people, by common consent, and the acceptance was solemnly ratified by sacrifice. In the 19th chapter of Exodus we read that God promised His people that if they would keep the covenant, He would make them "a peculiar treasure"; that is, His own special and private possession, "and ye shall be unto me a kingdom of priests and a holy nation." This is what Moses tried to teach the people. He tried to sanctify them through the Priesthood. See also 1 Pet. 2:9. The Saints of God are there referred to as a "holy Priesthood."

But Israel did not keep the covenant, and the result was that Moses was taken from them, and with him the greater Priesthood.

It was, as Paul calls the Law (Gal. 3:24), "our schoolmaster to bring us to Christ." It was confined to one tribe, that of Levi, and the presidency was vested in one family, that of Aaron. Hence its name, the Aaronic, or Levitic Priesthood.

"The Children of Israel were not capable of living up to all the requirements of the Higher or Holy Priesthood and the law of the Gospel, so the Lord, through Moses, gave them a new law and order of the Holy Priesthood, and another set of officers to administer to the people under the new conditions. . . .

"This new authority, or new Priesthood, or rather this new adaptation of and order of the old Priesthood, is called the 'Lesser Priesthood.' It is an appendage of the Higher Priesthood, because it belongs to or grows out of it." (Joseph B. Keeler, *"The Lesser Priesthood,"* p. 8.)

The Lord had promised to Israel that if the people would obey His voice he would make of them a royal Priesthood, and He would give them the fulness of the Priesthood and the Gospel, but they hardened their hearts against him.

Through Moses he said: "Now, therefore, if ye will obey my voice indeed, and keep my covenant, then ye shall be a peculiar treasure unto me above all people: for all the earth is mine. And ye shall be unto me a kingdom of Priests (i.e. of the Melchizedek order), and an holy nation.

These are the words which thou shalt speak unto the children of Israel."
(Ex. 19:5-6.) "But they hardened their hearts and could not endure His
presence, therefore, the Lord in his wrath, for his anger was kindled
against them, swore that they should not enter into his rest while in the
wilderness, which rest is the fulness of his glory." (V. 24.) This Aaronic
Priesthood was to remain with them until the coming of Christ in his
ministry.

The mission of the Aaronic Priesthood is here stated. It holds the key
to the gospel of repentance, baptism, the remission of sins, and the Law of
Carnal Commandments—the Law which was in force until John the
Baptist. (Hyrum M. Smith and Janne M. Sjodahl, *Doctrine and Covenants
Commentary,* Deseret Book Co., 1972, pp. 502-3.)

President Joseph Fielding Smith, in his *Way to Perfection,* says:

There have been times in the history of the world when these ordinances could not be given, for there were no authorized servants holding
the Priesthood among the people. Millions of worthy souls have died
without relief from their sins and without knowing of the Gospel, who
would have received all these commandments if the opportunity had been
extended to them. Even the children of Israel—with whom the Lord made
covenants through their fathers Abraham and Israel—were left for
centuries without the fulness of these blessings.

When the Lord took Moses out of their midst, he took the Melchizedek Priesthood also, and left the Aaronic Priesthood with the preparatory Gospel, and to this was attached the law. This was done because the
anger of the Lord was kindled against the people for their hardness of
heart. The Lord "swore that they should not enter into his rest while in the
wilderness, which rest is the fulness of his glory." (D&C 84:24.)

These Israelites could not, therefore, obtain the fulness of the blessings. Just what ordinances were given them, beyond the preparatory
Gospel, we do not know. That they were restricted is apparent, so they
were unable to obtain the blessings which would entitle them to a "fulness
of his glory." It was necessary because of this for these ancient people to
wait until the time should come when others could act for them. This time
came after the resurrection of our Lord. (Salt Lake City: Deseret Book
Co., 1975, pp. 174-75.)

Chapter 16

MOSES AND AARON

The appointment of Aaron and his sons to the ministry carries with it some interesting and important lessons.

It all began, of course, with the call of Moses. At first Aaron seems not to have been included in the consideration at all.

The third chapter of Exodus gives the detail of the Lord's first call to Moses when, from a burning bush, the divine voice called out: "Moses, Moses," to which he replied, "Here am I."

Telling Moses to remove his shoes because the ground there had been made holy, the Lord identified himself: "I am the God of thy father, the God of Abraham, the God of Isaac, and the God of Jacob. And Moses hid his face; for he was afraid to look upon God." (Exodus 3:6.)

This identification of himself by the Lord is interesting also in view of a similar statement made subsequently by the Almighty to his servant: "And God spake unto Moses, and said unto him, I am the Lord: And I appeared unto Abraham, unto Isaac, and unto Jacob, by the name of God Almighty, but by my name JEHOVAH was I not known to them." (Exodus 6:2-3.)

This is most interesting in view of the Lord's identification to Joseph Smith, as recorded in D&C 110:3-4, wherein we read: ". . . and his voice was as the sound of the rushing of great waters, even the voice of Jehovah, saying: I am the first and the last; I am he who liveth, I am he who was slain; I am your advocate with the Father."

Important also in this connection is 3 Nephi wherein the Savior himself says that he gave the law to Moses. (3 Nephi 15:2-10.)

Although Moses was told definitely that it was the

Almighty speaking to him, the prophet hesitated and protested that he was not able to do the work required. "Now the man Moses was very meek, above all the men which were upon the face of the earth." (Numbers 12:3.)

"Who am I, that I should go unto Pharaoh?" he asked the Lord, feeling his great inadequacy.

He argued in the same way when the Lord asked him to go to the elders of Israel about their impending release from bondage. "They will not believe me" was his argument. (Exodus 4:1.)

The Lord had said: "They shall hearken to thy voice." (Exodus 3:18.) He offered miracles as persuaders. But even this did not satisfy the timid shepherd who was now being called to be a prophet.

So "Moses said unto the Lord, O my Lord, I am not eloquent, neither heretofore, nor since thou hast spoken unto thy servant: but I am slow of speech, and of a slow tongue." (Exodus 4:10.)

This angered the Lord, who replied: "Who hath made man's mouth, or who maketh the dumb, or deaf, or the seeing, or the blind? Have not I the Lord?" (Exodus 4:11.) Then he said to Moses: "Go, and I will be with thy mouth, and teach thee what thou shalt say." (Exodus 4:12.)

Even this promise of eloquence did not satisfy Moses, who insisted on having someone else to help him.

"And the anger of the Lord was kindled against Moses, and he said, Is not Aaron the Levite thy brother? I know that he can speak well." And so Aaron was called. "And he shall be thy spokesman unto the people, and he shall be, even he shall be to thee instead of a mouth." (Exodus 4:14-16.)

So this was the first call of Aaron, and it came by revelation from God. Even in this preliminary work, prior to his call to the ministry, he was called by revelation.

The Lord would have made Moses eloquent if he had but accepted the divine word. He would have made his humble servant equal to every situation. "Is any thing too hard for the Lord?" (Genesis 18:14.)

But the Lord was patient, and he gave Moses the help of Aaron in approaching Pharaoh and releasing Israel.

However, there was still another calling awaiting Aaron. This came after the people had arrived in the wilderness and when an organization for the ministry was being considered.

It will be remembered that a portable tabernacle was required by the Lord for sacred services, as were various types of sacrifices and burnt offerings. Priestly administration was essential to this labor. Temple service has always been administered by the priesthood, and the tabernacle was but a forerunner of the temple. Sacred ordinances were performed therein.

Aaron and his sons were now called to serve in the priests' offices. We read: "And take thou unto thee Aaron thy brother, and his sons with him, from among the children of Israel, that he may minister unto me in the priest's office, even Aaron, Nadab and Abihu, Eleazar and Ithamar, Aaron's sons." (Exodus 28:1.)

Following the call, instructions were given regarding their work and their apparel, that they "may minister unto me in the priest's office."

The apostle Paul spoke of Aaron's call as he referred to the holy priesthood, and said: "And no man taketh this honour unto himself, but he that is called of God, as was Aaron." (Hebrews 5:4.)

Since this is such an important point, it may be of interest to note the renderings of this scripture in some other translations of the Bible.

The New English Bible says: "And nobody arrogates this honor to himself: he is called by God, as indeed Aaron was."

The Revised Standard Version: "And one does not take the honor upon himself, but he is called by God just as Aaron was."

The Knox Catholic Bible: "His vocation comes from God, as Aaron's did; nobody can take on himself such a privilege as this."

The Moffatt Version: "It is an office which no one elects to take for himself; he is called to it by God, just as Aaron was."

The point is that God is to select his own ministers; no one assumes the call for himself. The manner in which it is made is to be like the call of Aaron; that is, by revelation from God to and through a living prophet, who in turn, with such authorization, calls a man to the ministry.

This same process was followed when Aaron was about to die and the Lord selected Eleazar, Aaron's son, to succeed him. (Numbers 20:23-29.)

During his own mortal ministry the Savior made this vital principle clear: "Ye have not chosen me," he said to his disciples, "but I have chosen you, and ordained you, that ye should go and bring forth fruit. . . ." (John 15:16.)

Here is a basic principle in the ministry of Christ's church. Men must be called of God by revelation to and through a living prophet, which means that there must always be current revelation and living prophets in the Lord's true church; otherwise no ministers are called of God.

Amos said: "Surely the Lord God will do nothing, but he revealeth his secret unto his servants the prophets." (Amos 3:7.)

Therefore God would not act in his church without the services of a prophet, not even so much as to call a man to the ministry. Prophets were in the church for the work of the ministry (Ephesians 4:12), and calling men to serve with divine authority most certainly is part of the ministry.

Paul asked the Romans: "How then shall they call on him in whom they have not believed? and how shall they believe in him of whom they have not heard? and how shall they hear without a preacher, *and how shall they preach, except they be sent?*" (Romans 10:14-15.)

When Moses' work was nearly finished, a successor was to be chosen to lead the Israelites over Jordan and into the Promised Land. Who should it be? The Lord solved the problem in the same manner as when Aaron was chosen. By direct revelation to the living prophet, Joshua was divinely called. Moses did not appoint him. God issued the call:

And the Lord said unto Moses, Take thee Joshua the son of Nun, a man in whom is the spirit, and lay thine hand upon him;
And set him before Eleazar the priest, and before all the congregation; and give him a charge in their sight. . . .
And Moses did as the Lord commanded him: and he took Joshua, and set him before Eleazar the priest, and before all the congregation:

And he laid his hands upon him, and gave him a charge, as the Lord commanded by the hands of Moses. (Numbers 27: 18-22.)

And further we read: "And Joshua the son of Nun was full of the spirit of wisdom; *for Moses had laid his hands upon him:* and the children of Israel hearkened unto him, and did as the Lord commanded Moses." (Deuteronomy 34:9.)

This is an inescapable principle with reference to the ministry of Christ. It is one of the signs of the true church. Where there is no revelation, where there are no prophets, men are not called to the ministry by the Lord.

If ministers are not called of God as was Aaron, their acts are not valid. The scripture has various accounts of the punishment that God has dealt out to those who have officiated without authority. Here then is one of the great lessons to be learned from the relationship of Aaron and Moses.

Appropriate to this theme is a portion of the Sermon on the Mount. The Lord had said:

> Not every one that saith unto me, Lord, Lord, shall enter into the kingdom of heaven; but he that doeth the will of my Father which is in heaven.
> Many will say to me in that day, Lord, Lord, have we not prophesied in thy name? and in thy name have cast out devils? and in thy name done many wonderful works?
> And then will I profess unto them, I never knew you: depart from me, ye that work iniquity. (Matthew 7:21-23.)

When Hugh J. Schonfield made his translation known as the *Authentic New Testament,* he gave this rendering: "Many will say to me at that time, 'Master, Master, have we not prophesied in your name, . . . and in your name performed many miracles?' But then I shall tell them plainly, 'I have never authorized you. Be off with you, you illegal practitioners!' " (Great Britain: Dobson Books Ltd., 1956, p. 51.)

Chapter 17

MOSES AND THE LAW

The gospel of the Lord Jesus Christ was taught to Adam and his family and is intended for all mankind. The early patriarchs and prophets, such as Enoch and Abraham, lived it and preached it.

At times great success rewarded their efforts, as in the case of Enoch (Moses 7) and Melchizedek (Alma 13). At other times the results were not so fruitful, as Paul indicated when he said: "For unto us was the gospel preached, as well as unto them: but the word preached did not profit them, not being mixed with faith in them that heard it." (Hebrews 4:2.)

Paul expressly said that the gospel was preached to Abraham. (Galatians 3:8.) Of this matter Peter also wrote:

Of which salvation the prophets have inquired and searched diligently, who prophesied of the grace that should come unto you:

Searching what, or what manner of time the Spirit of Christ which was in them did signify, when it testified beforehand the sufferings of Christ, and the glory that should follow. (1 Peter 1:10-11.)

During their 430-year stay in Egypt the children of Israel became apostate and began to follow after the ways of that idolatrous land; hence the occurrence involving the golden calf.

Paul, writing to the Hebrews, discussed them:

Harden not your hearts, as in the provocation, in the day of temptation in the wilderness:

When your fathers tempted me, proved me, and saw my works forty years.

Wherefore I was grieved with that generation, and said, They do always err in their heart; and they have not known my ways.

So I sware in my wrath, They shall not enter into my rest.

Take heed, brethren, lest there be in any of you an evil heart of unbelief, in departing from the living God.

For some, when they had heard, did provoke: howbeit not all that came out of Egypt by Moses.

But with whom was he grieved forty years? was it not with them that had sinned, whose carcases fell in the wilderness?

And to whom sware he that they should not enter into his rest, but to them that believed not?

So we see that they could not enter in because of unbelief. (Hebrews 3:8-12, 16-19.)

So, as Paul said, those who came out of Egypt could not enter the Promised Land because of their unbelief. The Lord allowed the forty years to go by to permit a new generation to arise, and it was this new generation that crossed over Jordan.

Moses had hoped that he could convert them to the gospel. He held the Melchizedek Priesthood; he was their prophet-leader, their revelator and seer. But many even of the new generation would not listen to him. They had been influenced too much by the evil examples of their parents as they had journeyed in the wilderness.

The result was that Israel, even after the screening process that went on in the wilderness, was not yet ready to accept the true God and live the beautiful truths of the gospel of Christ.

But the Lord was infinitely patient. He would keep his covenant with Abraham. He had promised the patriarch that Palestine would be the homeland of his children, and likewise that through his family all nations of the earth would be blessed. That of course meant that faith in the true God must be preserved.

The Lord then determined that he would give the tribes a preparatory course of lesser commandments as a foundation upon which they could build an acceptance of the higher laws.

The people were selfish. Evidently many of them were depraved, judging from the types of laws included in the new plan. In view of this, a stern correction of these traits was required.

To make the commandments strict, the Lord brought in the death penalty for disobedience in many cases, and in doing so he made it clear that the righteous must not feel sorry for those suffering the extreme penalty, for they had brought it upon themselves. (Deuteronomy 19:13.)

To illustrate the manner in which this new law, known as the law of Moses, served as a schoolmaster, it will be noted that the Lord mixed in with the carnal commandments some of the most important of the higher laws.

The first and great commandment, to love the Lord with all our heart, soul, and strength, is basic in any dispensation of the gospel. As given then it read:

Hear, O Israel: the Lord our God is one Lord:
And thou shalt love the Lord thy God with all thine heart, and with all thy soul, and with all thy might.
And these words, which I command thee this day, shall be in thine heart:
And thou shalt teach them diligently unto thy children, and shalt talk of them when thou sittest in thine house, and when thou walkest by the way, and when thou liest down, and when thou risest up.
And thou shalt bind them for a sign upon thine hand, and they shall be as frontlets between thine eyes.
And thou shalt write them upon the posts of thy house, and on thy gates. (Deuteronomy 6:4-9.)

Later, as Moses addressed the congregation, he said: "And now, Israel, what doth the Lord thy God require of thee, but to fear the Lord thy God, to walk in all his ways, and to love him, and to serve the Lord thy God with all thy heart and with all thy soul?" (Deuteronomy 10:12.)

He continually emphasized the thought of one Lord and one God, the God of Abraham, Isaac, and Jacob, thus to draw their minds away from the polyglot of paganistic Egyptian practices with their gods of gold and stone and water, and of the moon and the sun.

It is interesting that at this early time he also held up to them the ultimate goal of becoming perfect like God; he said: "Thou shalt be perfect with the Lord thy God." (Deuteronomy 18:13.)

This command came after his condemnation of all kinds of wizardry that he branded as abominations before the Lord. It was because of their false religions, as well as their depravity, that the Lord was driving the Canaanites out of the land. He would use the Israelites as his instruments in doing so, but Israel must not become contaminated by the people they were to destroy!

The Revised Version of the Bible reads as follows: "For

anyone given to these practices is abominable to the Lord; indeed it is because of these abominable practices that the Lord your God is driving them out of your way. You must be absolutely true to the Lord your God; for while these nations whom you are to conquer give heed to soothsayers and diviners, the Lord your God has not intended you to do so." (Deuteronomy 18:9-15.)

The Israelites were in this peculiar position: Behind them were the pagan gods of the Egyptians. Before them were the equally pagan gods of the Canaanites, whose practices included witchery, wizardry, and "peeping and muttering mediums" who held seances and pretended to call up the dead. It was all an abomination to the Lord.

Therefore he was stern and strict in this matter, and made it a capital offense to worship in these errant ways. Such worship was apostasy from the truth, and if handed down to other generations it could thwart the promises of the Lord to Abraham. The Lord could not be lenient on this point. And anyway, who can achieve any degree of perfection by imperfect means?

Among the higher laws mixed with the carnal commandments were also many that in detail taught the overall principle of the Golden Rule, to do unto others as we would be done by.

So the "schoolmaster" combined the lesser law with some principles of the higher law to keep their goals in proper focus, even though the Melchizedek Priesthood and Moses the prophet were removed from them.

Paul explained this to the Galatians as he attempted to show them how Christ's gospel, brought by the Savior himself, did away with the carnal commandments:

But before faith came, we were kept under the law, shut up unto the faith which should afterwards be revealed.

Wherefore the law was our schoolmaster to bring us unto Christ, that we might be justified by faith.

But after that faith is come, we are no longer under a schoolmaster.

For ye are all the children of God by faith in Christ Jesus.

For as many of you as have been baptized into Christ have put on Christ.

There is neither Jew nor Greek, there is neither bond nor free, there is neither male nor female: for ye are all one in Christ Jesus.

And if ye be Christ's, then are ye Abraham's seed, and heirs according to the promise. (Galatians 3:23-29.)

But basic to it all was a knowledge of and a firm belief in the true God. The Israelites had been so exposed to idolatry in Egypt that many wavered and quite obviously lost the true concept of God. Otherwise they would not have worshiped so willingly before Aaron's golden calf.

If the Lord was to save them, he must first teach them the truth about himself. He must allow them to know in no uncertain terms that he lives, that he is a Person, that Jehovah is his name, and that the pagan deities are nothing but dumb idols made of stone or silver or gold. (3 Nephi 15; Leviticus 6.)

Chapter 18

THE REVELATION OF GOD

No one can worship God intelligently without an accurate understanding of the nature of the Deity. It is a lack of such knowledge that leads people into false religions and self-conceived creeds. They grope in the dark.

This was true of the ancient Israelites, contaminated as they were by idolatry and sin. It is true also today, which is one of the reasons for the proliferation of creeds and sects in the so-called Christian world.

It was the case in the early days of the Prophet Joseph Smith, when religious revivals emphasized the point to such a degree that the young prophet required divine wisdom to escape confusion.

In his day no one knew what God was like. Therefore, as a prerequisite to the restoration of the gospel, it must needs be that the correct knowledge of God be restored to provide a firm foundation upon which the restored Church could be built.

Hence the first vision of the Prophet Joseph, wherein he was permitted to see our Eternal Heavenly Father and his Son, Jesus the Christ, our Mediator and Redeemer. He discovered that indeed they were in human form, and that the scripture was correct in saying that man was made in the image and likeness of God.

He heard their voices and received their counsel. And as he gazed upon them he could see plainly two heavenly Personages, and he knew for a fact that they were as separate and distinct as any two other persons, each one an individual by himself.

At that moment, for the first time in many centuries, a mortal human being knew what God looked like, and heard his spoken words. It was only with this sure knowledge that Joseph Smith was able to proceed with his great assignment.

Knowing that God is real, the Prophet also came to know that Moroni, a man who came back from the dead as a heavenly messenger, was also real; that the Book of Mormon plates were real; and that the entire restoration procedure was factual, substantial, literal, corporeal, and physical— everything being a complete *reality*.

A sure knowledge of the nature of God was needed also by the ancient Israelites, who were steeped in the idolatrous ways of the Egyptians. What did they know about the true God?

For four centuries they had seen the worship of images of stone or wood that were manufactured before their own eyes, and they knew that all such were merely human creations. But because the Egyptians worshiped those articles and had such faith in them, the Israelites acquired a similar faith. Hence the golden calf episode, which so upset both the Lord and Moses.

In their ignorance the Israelites worshiped the calf. In their ignorance they were swayed toward Egyptian beliefs. And in their ignorance they doubted Moses and complained even when great miracles were performed on their behalf. No wonder the Prophet Joseph said that no one can be saved in ignorance!

Knowing about God through some personal contact would provide a firsthand understanding of him. As they were taught further about him, their knowledge would give them a purpose in life and goals for them to accomplish. This new knowledge revealed that they could even become like the true and living God, actually perfect. No pagan religion could do that for them.

The Almighty recognized this need and proceeded to make himself known to the people in general, so "the Lord came down upon mount Sinai, on the top of the mount: and the Lord called Moses up to the top of the mount; and Moses went up." (Exodus 19:20.)

The Lord explained to Moses that the people must be kept back some distance from the mount, and their priests also, because by coming too near they might be consumed by the glory of his appearance.

Then God spoke "all these words, saying, I am the Lord

thy God, which have brought thee out of the land of Egypt, out of the house of bondage. *Thou shalt have no other gods before me."* (Exodus 20:1-3. Italics added.)

The Lord then proceeded to give the Ten Commandments, which he also engraved on stone with his own finger. His words were accompanied by thunder and lightning, a dramatic demonstration of divine power. It frightened the people, who now were convinced of the reality of God. They feared to come close to him, and sought only to have Moses act as their intermediary.

> And all the people saw the thunderings, and the lightnings, and the noise of the trumpet, and the mountain smoking: and when the people saw it, they removed, and stood afar off.
>
> And they said unto Moses, Speak thou with us, and we will hear: but let not God speak with us, lest we die.
>
> And Moses said unto the people, Fear not: for God is come to prove you, and that his fear may be before your faces, that ye sin not.
>
> And the Lord said unto Moses, Thus thou shalt say unto the children of Israel, Ye have seen that I have talked with you from heaven.
>
> Ye shall not make with me gods of silver, neither shall ye make unto you gods of gold. (Exodus 20:18-20, 22-23.)

The Lord stressed this point: *"Ye have seen that I have talked with you from heaven.* Ye shall not make with me gods of silver, neither shall ye make unto you gods of gold." (Exodus 20:22-23. Italics added.)

The Revised Version of the Bible puts it like this: "The Lord said to Moses, Thus shall you say to the Israelites, *You have seen for yourselves that I have talked with you out of heaven.* Gods of silver and gods of gold you must not make for yourselves."

The Jerusalem Bible says: "Yahweh said to Moses, 'Tell the sons of Israel this, *"You have seen for yourselves that I have spoken to you from heaven.* You shall not make gods of silver or gods of gold to stand beside me. You shall not make things like this for yourselves." ' "

To further prove his existence and to teach the people of his reality, the Lord called the seventy elders of Israel to ascend the mount with Moses and Aaron and come into the divine presence. Although the people at large were frightened and lacked sufficient faith to see God themselves, the Lord was willing that their representatives, the seventy elders of Israel, see him; they could then testify to the people of what they had seen.

> Then went up Moses, and Aaron, Nadab, and Abihu, and seventy of the elders of Israel:
> And they saw the God of Israel: and there was under his feet as it were a paved work of a sapphire stone, and as it were the body of heaven in his clearness.
> And upon the nobles of the children of Israel he laid not his hand: also they saw God, and did eat and drink. (Exodus 24:9-11.)

What more could the Lord have done in convincing them? These elders came into his real presence. They saw him clearly, and they "did eat and drink." The reality of this whole experience was beyond any question.

With Moses the reality was even greater. He saw and visited with God personally and directly. He dwelt with him for a period of forty days and nights. During this entire time he neither ate nor drank. (Deuteronomy 9:9-18.) Not only did he see the Lord face to face, but at another time, he saw "his back parts" (Exodus 33:11-23) when his face was not disclosed.

Moses became so companionable with the Lord that he actually argued with him, persuading the Lord at one time not to destroy the errant Israelites. This was occasioned by the worship of the golden calf, when Aaron temporarily went astray. The Lord was very angry with the people over this, and said to Moses: "Now therefore let me alone, that my wrath may wax hot against them, and that I may consume them: and I will make of thee a great nation." (Exodus 32:10.)

Since the people were so disobedient and lacking in faith, the Lord apparently considered destroying them and starting afresh to raise up a righteous people through the loins of Moses. Since the prophet was a descendant of Abraham, the promises could still be fulfilled through his lineage as effectively as through any of the other tribes.

But responding to the importunities of Moses, the Lord withdrew his wrath.

> And Moses besought the Lord his God, and said, Lord, why doth thy wrath wax hot against thy people, which thou hast brought forth out of the land of Egypt with great power, and with a mighty hand?

Wherefore should the Egyptians speak, and say, For mischief did he bring them out, to slay them in the mountains, and to consume them from the face of the earth? Turn from thy fierce wrath, and repent of this evil against thy people.

Remember Abraham, Isaac, and Israel, thy servants, to whom thou swarest by thine own self, and saidst unto them, I will multiply your seed as the stars of heaven, and all this land that I have spoken of will I give unto your seed, and they shall inherit it for ever.

And the Lord repented of the evil which he thought to do unto his people. (Exodus 32:11-14.)

Moses had broken the first tablets in dismay over the golden calf incident, so now the Lord agreed to give him a new set.

And the Lord said unto Moses, Hew thee two tables of stone like unto the first: and I will write upon these tables the words that were in the first tables, which thou brakest.

And be ready in the morning, and come up in the morning unto mount Sinai, and present thyself there to me in the top of the mount.

And no man shall come up with thee, neither let any man be seen throughout all the mount; neither let the flocks nor herds feed before that mount.

And he hewed two tables of stone like unto the first; and Moses rose up early in the morning, and went up unto mount Sinai, as the Lord had commanded him, and took in his hand the two tables of stone.

And the Lord descended in the cloud, and stood with him there, and proclaimed the name of the Lord.

And the Lord passed by before him, and proclaimed, The Lord, The Lord God, merciful and gracious, longsuffering, and abundant in goodness and truth,

Keeping mercy for thousands, forgiving iniquity and transgression and sin, and that will by no means clear the guilty; visiting the iniquity of the fathers upon the children, and upon the children's children, unto the third and to the fourth generation.

And Moses made haste, and bowed his head toward the earth, and worshipped.

And he said, If now I have found grace in thy sight, O Lord, let my Lord, I pray thee, go among us; for it is a stiffnecked people; and pardon our iniquity and our sin, and take us for thine inheritance. (Exodus 34:1-9.)

The Lord then covenanted with Moses to bring the people into the Promised Land, but it was stipulated that the wicked peoples already living in that land must be destroyed, together with their images. But the Lord warned:

Take heed to thyself, lest thou make a covenant with the inhabitants of the land whither thou goest, lest it be for a snare in the midst of thee:

But ye shall destroy their altars, break their images, and cut down their groves:

For thou shalt worship no other god: for the Lord, whose name is Jealous, is a jealous God:

Lest thou make a covenant with the inhabitants of the land, and they go a whoring after their gods, and do sacrifice unto their gods, and one call thee, and thou eat of his sacrifice;

And thou take of their daughters unto thy sons, and their daughters go a whoring after their gods, and make thy sons go a whoring after their gods.

Thou shalt make thee no molten gods. (Exodus 34:12-17.)

The Pearl of Great Price account of God's personal dealings with Moses further demonstrates the fact of the reality of the Lord and fully confirms the Bible in this matter.

Chapter 19

THE TEN COMMANDMENTS

By his own finger the Lord wrote the Ten Commandments on tablets of stone. They represent the basic law of the Almighty and have formed the underlying elements of civil and religious law ever since.

They are fundamental to our relationships with God. They are an integral part of the restored gospel of the Lord Jesus Christ and are essential to our becoming perfect as our Father in heaven is perfect. (D&C 42; D&C 59.)

Variations of these laws are given in the rules laid down in Leviticus and Deuteronomy as they are applied to specific matters, but generally they form the foundation for all proper human conduct.

As we read the Sermon on the Mount we see again many of the same important principles of human relationships expressed there. This is not surprising when it is remembered that the same God—Jesus of Nazareth, the Jehovah of the Old Testament—gave us both. Two great principles cover all aspects of these laws: one is devotion to the only true and living God; the other is the operation of the Golden Rule, that we do to others as we would be done by.

The Ten Commandments, the Sermon on the Mount, and the other teachings of Jesus all bear testimony that the gospel is unchanging, that salvation is the same for all peoples in all ages, and that they form the pattern by which we may become Christlike in our lives.

In commenting upon the Ten Commandments, President Heber J. Grant said: "No commandment was ever given to us but what God has given us the power to keep that commandment."

President Brigham Young said: "The commandments of God are given to us expressly for our benefit, and if we live in obedience to them we shall live so as to understand the mind and will of God for ourselves, and concerning ourselves as individuals." (*Journal of Discourses* 12:126.)

Proper observance of the Ten Commandments would eliminate crime, war, and immorality in all their forms. It would likewise build up a people so devoted to the Almighty that they could become like those in the City of Enoch. They would be fully acceptable to the Lord.

The First Commandment

"Thou shalt have no other gods before me." (Exodus 20:3.)

God will not favor us if we put him in second place in our lives and if we follow after worldly things regardless of what they may be.

The command of the Savior was: "Seek ye first the kingdom of God, and his righteousness." (Matthew 6:33.) In revelations to the Prophet Joseph Smith the Lord taught that we must have an eye single to the glory of God. (D&C 27:2; 55:1; 59:1; 88:67.)

The Lord did two things in giving us this first of the Ten Commandments: he prohibited the use of images and idols in his worship, and he taught us that we must concentrate our attention on worshiping him and thereby becoming like him.

In the Sermon on the Mount the Savior made it abundantly clear that we "cannot serve God and mammon." (Matthew 6:24.) He will accept no divided allegiance from any of us. That is why the first and great commandment is both first and great: "Thou shalt love the Lord thy God with all thy heart, and with all thy soul, and with all thy mind." (Matthew 22:37.)

As he gave it to the Prophet Joseph Smith in modern revelation, it was expressed in terms of service to the Lord: "O ye that embark in the service of God, see that ye serve him with all your heart, might, mind and strength, that ye may stand blameless before God at the last day." (D&C 4:2.)

The command is as binding on us of today as it was upon ancient Israel. It is possible for us to have our false gods also.

They may or may not be in the shape of idols or images; they may be in the form of money or business or pleasure or sin. The command is applicable to everyone.

The Lord made abundantly clear what he expects of his people, for he said: "Ye shall be holy: for I the Lord your God am holy." (Leviticus 19:2.) This applied to ancient Israel and it applies likewise to modern Israel. If we are to become like God, then it goes without saying that we must be holy as he is; and we cannot do this if we follow after the gods of this world.

The Second Commandment

"Thou shalt not make unto thee any graven image, or any likeness of any thing that is in heaven above, or that is in the earth beneath, or that is in the water under the earth:

"Thou shalt not bow down thyself to them, nor serve them: for I the Lord thy God am a jealous God, visiting the iniquity of the fathers upon the children unto the third and fourth generation of them that hate me;

"And shewing mercy unto thousands of them that love me, and keep my commandments." (Exodus 20:4-6.)

Here the Lord comes to grips with the immediate problem that faced the Israelites. They had been taught idolatry by the Egyptians. They were now to enter the Promised Land, which was inhabited by another idolatrous people. They were warned against the Egyptian religions, but they must likewise be forewarned against the evils they would find in Canaan.

Every idol represented a false god. Every idol likewise represented an entirely false religion, a false philosophy, a mistaken concept of both God himself and his relationship to man. Hence they must be banished forever.

To make it clear that this related directly to the use of images in worship, the Lord specified: "Thou shalt not bow down thyself to them, nor serve them." (Leviticus 20:5.)

When the Lord spoke in Leviticus he said: "Ye shall make you no idols nor graven image, neither rear you up a standing image, neither shall ye set up any image of stone in

your land, *to bow down unto it;* for I am the Lord your God."
(Leviticus 26:1. Italics added.)

Some people have supposed that these commandments
ruled out photographs or sculpture of any and all kinds. The
Lord does not make his commandment that broad. He says
we are not to make any image *to bow down unto it in worship.*
He brands such images as idols, and of course an idol is a
heathen god that is worshiped. "Thou shalt not bow down
thyself to them, *nor serve them.*"

Obviously he was making no reference to pictures we
might have of old Aunt Alice or of sculpture pieces of Wash-
ington or Lincoln. He is talking of using images *in worship,*
which is directly opposed to his law.

His reference to visiting the sins of the fathers upon the
children is an interesting one. Misunderstandings have
arisen over that passage, particularly when readers of the
scripture have failed to note the words: "of them that hate
me." He makes it plain in the verses that follow that he
blesses those who keep his commandments. The penalty is
for those who hate God.

President Joseph F. Smith discussed this point as
follows:

Infidels will say to you: "How unjust, how unmerciful, how unGod-
like it is to visit the iniquities of the parents upon the children of the third
and fourth generation of them that hate God." How do you see it? This
way: and it is strictly in accordance with God's law. The infidel will
impart infidelity to his children if he can. The whoremonger will not raise
a pure, righteous posterity. He will impart seeds of disease and misery, if
not of death and destruction, upon his offspring, which will continue upon
his children and descend to his children's children to the third and fourth
generation.

It is perfectly natural that the children should inherit from their
fathers, and if they sow the seeds of corruption, crime and loathsome disease, their children will reap the fruits thereof. Not in accordance with
God's wishes, for his wish is that men will not sin and therefore will not
transmit the consequences of their sin to their children, but that they will
keep his commandments, and be free from sin and from entailing the
effects of sin upon their offspring.

But inasmuch as men will not hearken unto the Lord, but will become a law unto themselves, and will commit sin, they will justly reap the
consequences of their own iniquity, and will naturally impart its fruits to
their children to the third and fourth generation.

The laws of nature are the laws of God who is just; it is not God that
inflicts these penalties, they are the effects of disobedience to his law. The

results of men's own acts follow them. (*Gospel Doctrine,* Deseret Book Co., 1975, pp. 401-2.)

Ezekiel makes the following explanation of this matter:

Yet say ye, Why? doth not the son bear the iniquity of the father? When the son hath done that which is lawful and right, and hath kept all my statutes, and hath done them, he shall surely live.

The soul that sinneth, it shall die. The son shall not bear the iniquity of the father, neither shall the father bear the iniquity of the son: the righteousness of the righteous shall be upon him, and the wickedness of the wicked shall be upon him.

But if the wicked will turn from all his sins that he hath committed, and keep all my statues, and do that which is lawful and right, he shall surely live, he shall not die.

All his transgressions that he hath committed, they shall not be mentioned unto him: in his righteousness that he hath done he shall live.

Have I any pleasure at all that the wicked should die? saith the Lord God: and not that he should return from his ways, and live?

But when the righteous turneth away from his righteousness, and committeth iniquity, and doeth according to all the abominations that the wicked man doeth, shall he live? All his righteousness that he hath done shall not be mentioned: in his trespass that he hath trespassed, and in his sin that he hath sinned, in them shall he die. (Ezekiel 18:19-24.)

He expands on it further in the thirty-third chapter of Ezekiel:

As I live, saith the Lord God, I have no pleasure in the death of the wicked; but that the wicked turn from his way and live: turn ye, turn ye from your evil ways; for why will ye die, O house of Israel?

Therefore, thou son of man, say unto the children of thy people, The righteousness of the righteous shall not deliver him in the day of his transgression: as for the wickedness of the wicked, he shall not fall thereby in the day that he turneth from his wickedness; neither shall the righteous be able to live for his righteousness in the day that he sinneth.

When I shall say to the righteous, that he shall surely live; if he trust to his own righteousness, and commit iniquity, all his righteousnesses shall not be remembered; but for his iniquity that he hath committed, he shall die for it.

Again, when I say unto the wicked, Thou shalt surely die; if he turn from his sin, and do that which is lawful and right;

If the wicked restore the pledge, give again that he had robbed, walk in the statutes of life, without committing iniquity; he shall surely live, he shall not die.

None of his sins that he hath committed shall be mentioned unto him: he hath done that which is lawful and right; he shall surely live.

Yet the children of thy people say, The way of the Lord is not equal: but as for them, their way is not equal.

When the righteous turneth from his righteousness, and committeth iniquity, he shall even die thereby.

But if the wicked turn from his wickedness, and do that which is lawful and right, he shall live thereby. (Ezekiel 33:11-19.)

In the Doctrine and Covenants we read: "Behold, he who has repented of his sins, the same is forgiven, and I, the Lord, remember them no more. By this ye may know if a man repenteth of his sins—behold, he will confess them and forsake them." (D&C 58:42-43.)

Amulek taught this to the Book of Mormon peoples:

Therefore, it is expedient that there should be a great and last sacrifice; and then shall there be, or it is expedient there should be, a stop to the shedding of blood; then shall the law of Moses be fulfilled; yea, it shall be all fulfilled, every jot and tittle, and none shall have passed away.

And behold, this is the whole meaning of the law, every whit pointing to that great and last sacrifice; and that great and last sacrifice will be the Son of God, yea, infinite and eternal.

And thus he shall bring salvation to all those who shall believe on his name; this being the intent of this last sacrifice, to bring about the bowels of mercy, which overpowereth justice, and bringeth about means unto men that they may have faith unto repentance.

And thus mercy can satisfy the demands of justice, and encircles them in the arms of safety, while he that exercises no faith unto repentance is exposed to the whole law of the demands of justice; therefore only unto him that has faith unto repentance is brought about the great and eternal plan of redemption. (Alma 34:13-16.)

The Third Commandment

"Thou shalt not take the name of the Lord thy God in vain; for the Lord will not hold him guiltless that taketh his name in vain." (Exodus 20:7.)

The name of the Lord should be spoken only in reverence. The ancient Jews hallowed it to the point where they did not even speak it at all. It was signified by the letters YHWH. Bible scholars use the term *Yahweh.*

To Latter-day Saints the name of the Lord is most sacred and significant. The names *Jehovah* and *Jesus Christ* both relate to the Savior alone. He is the divine Son of God. He is the Redeemer and the Messiah. And he was the Creator of all the worlds. Isaiah predicted that he would be called "Wonderful, Counseller, The mighty God, The everlasting Father, The Prince of Peace." (Isaiah 9:6.)

In Section 110 of the Doctrine and Covenants we have a straightforward declaration that Jesus is Jehovah. Peter made a significant statement about the Savior when he said:

Be it known unto you all, and to all the people of Israel, that by the name of Jesus Christ of Nazareth, whom ye crucified, whom God raised from the dead, even by him doth this man stand here before you whole.

This is the stone which was set at nought of you builders, which is become the head of the corner.

Neither is there salvation in any other: for there is none other name under heaven given among men, whereby we must be saved. (Acts 4:10-12.)

Paul writing to Timothy said:

For there is one God, and one mediator between God and men, the man Christ Jesus;

Who gave himself a ransom for all, to be testified in due time.

Whereunto I am ordained a preacher, and an apostle, (I speak the truth in Christ, and lie not;) a teacher of the Gentiles in faith and verity. (1 Timothy 2:5-7.)

Since we receive our salvation through him and in his name, since we perform our saving ordinances in his name, since we offer all of our prayers in his name, and since he is the mighty God and Creator of all, should we not reverence him and his name? Shall we affront him and jeopardize our salvation by taking his name in vain? Can we say we are "for" him if we thus insult him? (Matthew 12:30. See also 3 Nephi 27:5-9.)

He offers us matchless blessings if we will but serve him and pray to the Father in his name. Said he: "And in that day ye shall ask me nothing. Verily, verily, I say unto you, Whatsoever ye shall ask the Father in my name, he will give it you. Hitherto have ye asked nothing in my name: ask, and ye shall receive, that your joy may be full." (John 16:23-24.)

The Fourth Commandment

"Remember the sabbath day, to keep it holy.

"Six days shalt thou labour, and do all thy work:

"But the seventh day is the sabbath of the Lord thy God: in it thou shalt not do any work, thou, nor thy son, nor thy daughter, thy manservant, nor thy maidservant, nor thy cattle, nor thy stranger that is within thy gates:

"For in six days the Lord made heaven and earth, the sea, and all that in them is, and rested the seventh day: wherefore the Lord blessed the sabbath day, and hallowed it." (Exodus 20:8-11.)

Observance of the law of the Sabbath is vital to all true

followers of the Lord. It is a holy day and was made so in the creation. It was likewise continued as a sacred day when its observance was changed to the first day of the week in recognition of the resurrection of the Master. (Acts 20:7; Revelation 1:10.)

The Sabbath was given to us as a heavenly sign (a) that God lives; (b) that Israel is his people; (c) that a weekly day of rest and worship is required.

Note the words of the scripture:

Speak thou also unto the children of Israel, saying, Verily my sabbaths ye shall keep: for it is a sign between me and you throughout your generations; that ye may know that I am the Lord that doth sanctify you.

Ye shall keep the sabbath therefore; for it is holy unto you: every one that defileth it shall surely be put to death: for whosoever doeth any work therein, that soul shall be cut off from among his people.

Six days may work be done; but in the seventh is the sabbath of rest, holy to the Lord: whosoever doeth any work in the sabbath day, he shall surely be put to death.

Wherefore the children of Israel shall keep the sabbath, to observe the sabbath throughout their generations, for a perpetual covenant.

It is a sign between me and the children of Israel for ever: for in six days the Lord made heaven and earth, and on the seventh day he rested, and was refreshed. (Exodus 31:13-17.)

The Lord was so thoughtful in giving us this day of rest that he even had the domesticated animals in mind. (Exodus 23:12.)

The fact that it is a day of worship also is plainly confirmed in the revelations to the Prophet Joseph Smith. We read:

And that thou mayest more fully keep thyself unspotted from the world, thou shalt go to the house of prayer and offer up thy sacraments upon my holy day;

For verily this is a day appointed unto you to rest from your labors, and to pay thy devotions unto the Most High;

Nevertheless thy vows shall be offered up in righteousness on all days and at all times;

But remember that on this, the Lord's day, thou shalt offer thine oblations and thy sacraments unto the Most High, confessing thy sins unto thy brethren, and before the Lord.

And on this day thou shalt do none other thing, only let thy food be prepared with singleness of heart that thy fasting may be perfect, or, in other words, that thy joy may be full.

Verily, this is fasting and prayer, or in other words, rejoicing and prayer. (D&C 59:9-14.)

Dare we ignore such a commandment as that? "Thou shalt do none other thing. . . ."

Isaiah condemned pleasure seeking on the Sabbath. (Isaiah 58:13.)

Nehemiah condemned commercialism on that holy day. (Nehemiah 13:15-22.)

Anciently the Lord made violation of the Sabbath a capital offense, it was so important to him: "Six days shall work be done, but on the seventh day there shall be to you an holy day, a sabbath of rest to the Lord: whosoever doeth work therein shall be put to death." (Exodus 35:2.)

And yet today it is one of the most widely disregarded and violated of the Lord's great laws.

The Fifth Commandment

"Honour thy father and thy mother: that thy days may be long upon the land which the Lord thy God giveth thee." (Exodus 20:12.)

Some of the Israelites evidently were so unkind to their parents that the Lord invoked the death penalty for certain types of such cruelty: "And he that smiteth his father, or his mother, shall be surely put to death. And he that curseth his father, or his mother, shall surely be put to death." (Exodus 21:15, 17.)

What tremendous importance he placed upon respect for our parents! The tendency of the people to be thus unfair and unkind was in the Savior's mind when he said:

But he answered and said unto them, Why do ye also transgress the commandment of God by your tradition?

For God commanded, saying, Honour thy father and mother: and, He that curseth father or mother, let him die the death.

But ye say, Whosoever shall say to his father or his mother, It is a gift, by whatsoever thou mightest be profited by me;

And honour not his father or his mother, he shall be free. Thus have ye made the commandment of God of none effect by your tradition. (Matthew 15:3-6.)

President David O. McKay, speaking of this commandment, said at one time:

Let us cherish in our homes as we cherish the lives of our children themselves that word *honor* with all the synonyms—respect, reverence, veneration; honoring mother, honoring father, having them honor us as we honor and revere God our Eternal Father. Let the element of honor, devotion, reverence permeate the home life. (*Gospel Ideals,* Deseret Book Co., 1976, pp. 483-84.)

But President McKay also spoke of the need for parents to be worthy of such respect. Said he:

It is the duty of parents and of the Church not only to teach but also to *demonstrate* to young people that living a life of truth and moral purity brings joy and happiness, while violations of moral and social laws result only in dissatisfaction, sorrow, and, when carried to extreme, in degradation. (Ibid., p. 425.)

The Sixth Commandment

"Thou shalt not kill." (Exodus 20:13.)

In support of this commandment, the Lord gave us the following through the Prophet Joseph Smith: "Thou shalt not kill; and he that kills shall not have forgiveness in this world, nor in the world to come. And again, I say, thou shalt not kill; but he that killeth shall die." (D&C 42:18-19.)

He further said: "And it shall come to pass, that if any persons among you shall kill they shall be delivered up and dealt with according to the laws of the land; for remember that he hath no forgiveness; and it shall be proved according to the laws of the land." (D&C 42:79.)

Nephi said this: "And again, the Lord God hath commanded that men should not murder; that they should not lie; that they should not steal; that they should not take the name of the Lord their God in vain; that they should not envy; that they should not have malice; that they should not contend one with another; that they should not commit whoredoms; and that they should do none of these things; for whoso doeth them shall perish." (2 Nephi 26:32.)

Nephi said earlier: "Wo unto the murderer who deliberately killeth, for he shall die." (2 Nephi 9:35.)

It is clear from the scripture that the death penalty was provided to reinforce this important commandment. There are numerous references in other scriptures on this point, such as Genesis 9:6; Exodus 21:12-25; and Deuteronomy 19:11-13.

In connection with the commandment "Thou shalt not kill," some have inquired whether this applies to abortions. We quote here the statement of the First Presidency on abortion:

> The Church opposes abortion and counsels its members not to submit to, be a party to, or perform an abortion except in the rare cases where, in the opinion of competent medical counsel, the life or health of the woman is seriously endangered or where the pregnancy was caused by forcible rape and produces serious emotional trauma in the victim. Even then it should be done only after counseling with the local bishop or branch president and after receiving divine confirmation through prayer.
>
> Abortion is one of the most revolting and sinful practices in this day, when we are witnessing the frightening evidence of permissiveness leading to sexual immorality.
>
> Members of the Church guilty of being parties to the sin of abortion are subject to the disciplinary action of the councils of the Church as circumstances warrant. In dealing with this serious matter, it would be well to keep in mind the word of the Lord stated in the 59th Section of the Doctrine and Covenants, verse 6, "Thou shalt not steal; neither commit adultery, nor kill; nor do anything like unto it."
>
> As far as has been revealed, the sin of abortion is one for which a person may repent and gain forgiveness.

The Seventh Commandment

"Thou shalt not commit adultery." (Exodus 20:14.)

Sex is sacred to the Lord. It was required as part of his plan for the perpetuity of life. He provided for reproduction of the human species as for all other forms of life. But it must be done in his way to receive his blessing. It must be a part of holy matrimony, and must include the responsibility of properly rearing the children thus conceived.

"Multiply and replenish the earth," the Lord commanded Adam and Eve in the Garden of Eden. Without such reproduction, life on earth would come to an end.

But the process must not be prostituted. "Be ye clean that bear the vessels of the Lord," he has said on several occasions. (D&C 38:42; 88:86; 133:5.) Parents who bear children literally bear vessels of the Lord, for we are all his offspring.

Capital punishment for adultery was required by the Lord in the days of Moses: "And the man that committeth adultery with another man's wife, even he that committeth adultery with his neighbour's wife, the adulterer and the adulteress shall surely be put to death." (Leviticus 20:10.)

President Joseph F. Smith discoursed on the importance of good family life and the rearing of children in this wise:

I desire to emphasize this. I want the young men of Zion to realize that this institution of marriage is not a man-made institution. It is of God. It is honorable, and no man who is of marriageable age is living his religion who remains single. It is not simply devised for the convenience alone of man, to suit his own notions, and his own ideas; to marry and then divorce, to adopt and then to discard, just as he pleases. There are great consequences connected with it, consequences which reach beyond this present time, into all eternity, for thereby souls are begotten into the world, and men and women obtain their being in the world. Marriage is the preserver of the human race. Without it, the purposes of God would be frustrated; virtue would be destroyed to give place to vice and corruption, and the earth would be void and empty.

Neither are the relationships that exist, or should exist, between parents and children, and between children and parents, of an ephemeral nature, nor of a temporal character. They are of eternal consequence, reaching beyond the veil, in spite of all that we can do. The man, and the woman who are the agents, in the providence of God, to bring living souls into the world, are made before God and the heavens, as responsible for these acts as is God himself responsible for the works of his own hands, and for the revelation of his own wisdom. The man and the woman who engage in this ordinance of matrimony are engaging in something that is of such far-reaching character, and is of such vast importance, that thereby hangs life and death, and eternal increase. Thereupon depends eternal happiness, or eternal misery.

For this reason, God has guarded this sacred institution by the most severe penalties, and has declared that whosoever is untrue to the marriage relation, whosoever is guilty of adultery, shall be put to death. This is scriptural law, though it is not practiced today, because modern civilization does not recognize the laws of God in relation to the moral status of mankind. The Lord commanded, "Whosoever sheddeth innocent blood, by man shall his blood be shed." Thereby God has given the law. Life is an important thing. No man has any right to take life, unless God commanded it. The law of God as to violation of the marriage covenant is just as strict, and is on a parallel with law against murder notwithstanding the former is not carried out. (*Gospel Doctrine*, pp. 272-73.)

He said further:

And no man holding the Priesthood who is worthy and of age should remain unmarried. They should also teach that the law of chastity is one of the most vital importance, both to children, and to men and to women. It is a vitally important principle to the children of God in all their lives, from the cradle to the grave.

God has fixed dreadful penalties against the transgression of his law of chastity, of virtue, of purity. When the law of God shall be in force among men, they will be cut off who are not absolutely pure and unsoiled and spotless—both men and women. We expect the women to be pure, we expect them to be spotless and without blemish, and it is as necessary and important for man to be pure and virtuous as for woman; indeed, no woman would ever be other than pure if men were so. (Ibid., pp. 273-74.)

President Smith also said:

I believe that to a very large extent the fashions of the day, and especially the fashions of women, have a tendency to evil and not to virtue or
modesty, and I deplore that evident fact, for you see it on every hand.
(Ibid., p. 278.)

Sex activity among unmarried people, including the
younger generation, is regarded by the Lord as deeply
serious. There is no room for promiscuity among the people
of God. It is corrupting, demoralizing, and debasing from
every standpoint.

The Eighth Commandment

"Thou shalt not steal." (Exodus 20:15.)
Not only did the Lord give this law to ancient Israel; he
also repeated it for our day in these words: "Thou shalt not
steal; and he that stealeth and will not repent shall be cast
out." (D&C 42:20.)
He also said: "Thou shalt not steal; neither commit adultery, nor kill, nor do anything like unto it." (D&C 59:6.)

The Ninth Commandment

"Thou shalt not bear false witness against thy neighbour." (Exodus 20:16.)
When the Lord gave us this commandment in our day,
he was direct and to the point in the use of modern terms.
"Thou shalt not lie," he said, adding, "he that lieth and will
not repent shall be cast out"—that is, from the body of the
Saints. (D&C 42:21.)
He speaks at times of those who "love and make a lie,"
and tells of their eventual condemnation if they do not
repent. Not only are they subject to expulsion from the
Church if they do not repent, but they are also condemned to
go with the adulterers, the sorcerers, and other evil people in
the world to come. Following their punishment they will be
assigned to the telestial glory, the lowest of the three
kingdoms. Of those who go to the telestial glory the revelation says:
"These are they who are thrust down to hell. These are

they who shall not be redeemed from the devil until the last resurrection, until the Lord, even Christ the Lamb, shall have finished his work." (D&C 76:84-85.)

The Lord further describes those going to telestial glory in these words:

Last of all, these all are they who will not be gathered with the saints, to be caught up unto the church of the Firstborn, and received into the cloud.

These are they who are liars, and sorcerers, and adulterers, and whoremongers, and whosoever loves and makes a lie.

These are they who suffer the wrath of God on earth.

These are they who suffer the vengeance of eternal fire.

These are they who are cast down to hell and suffer the wrath of Almighty God, until the fulness of times, when Christ shall have subdued all enemies under his feet, and shall have perfected his work;

When he shall deliver up the kingdom, and present it unto the Father, spotless, saying: I have overcome and have trodden the wine-press alone, even the wine-press of the fierceness of the wrath of Almighty God. (D&C 76:102-7.)

To bear false witness is to lie. And what condemnation false witnesses shall receive! There were false witnesses at the trial of the Lord Jesus Christ. Can anyone measure the depth of their sin?

There were likewise false witnesses against the Prophet Joseph Smith, men who eventually contributed to his martyrdom and that of his brother Hyrum. Innocent blood was shed that day, and it is traced back to his enemies who also were false witnesses.

False witness is despised by the Lord. Note what we read in Proverbs:

These six things doth the Lord hate: yea, seven are an abomination unto him:

A proud look, a lying tongue, and hands that shed innocent blood,

An heart that deviseth wicked imaginations, feet that be swift in running to mischief,

A false witness that speaketh lies, and he that soweth discord among brethren. (Proverbs 6:16-19.)

The Tenth Commandment

"Thou shalt not covet thy neighbour's house, thou shalt not covet thy neighbour's wife, nor his manservant, nor his maidservant, nor his ox, nor his ass, nor any thing that is thy neighbour's." (Exodus 20:17.)

Paul speaks of "thou shalt not covet" in terms of lust. (Romans 7:7.) In many cases it is just that. The dictionary confirms this also and says that one who covets is one who lusts or has excessive desires for that which belongs to someone else.

The scripture says that we must not covet anything that is "thy neighbour's." It makes particular mention of "thy neighbour's wife," which equally includes "thy neighbour's husband."

To break up another's home and steal the father or mother of that home is indeed a despicable act. Yet it is done often these days. In fact, if we examine the divorce records we would think it is almost reaching epidemic proportions.

What does modern revelation say about it? Note the words of the Lord:

> Thou shalt love thy wife with all thy heart, and shalt cleave unto her and none else.
> And he that looketh upon a woman to lust after her shall deny the faith, and shall not have the Spirit; and if he repents not he shall be cast out.
> Thou shalt not commit adultery; and he that committeth adultery, and repenteth not, shall be cast out.
> But he that has committed adultery and repents with all his heart, and forsaketh it, and doeth it no more, thou shalt forgive;
> But if he doeth it again, he shall not be forgiven, but shall be cast out. (D&C 42:22-26.)

If only the Latter-day Saints would read carefully that command, for such it is, and note especially the "none else" portion, many homes would be spared.

Every man is commanded by the Almighty to love his wife with all his heart, and to cleave unto her—and to none else! The command applies equally to the wife.

When the Lord speaks of "cleaving unto her," he is speaking of the constant courtship that President McKay said should continue all through life between husband and wife. We must all work at our marriages to make them succeed, and one of the most effective things in this regard is to live the Golden Rule. If every husband were to treat his wife as he himself would like to be treated, and if every wife were to treat her husband as she herself would like to be treated, wouldn't every marriage be made into a heavenly experience? Divorce never would be known in such cases. A large percent of broken homes result from coveting someone else's partner.

Coveting property or money is at the bottom of nearly all crime. Wars between nations arise because of coveting. Evil craving for sex is at the bottom of every case of fornication, adultery, and homosexual activity. Shoplifting, one of our most common crimes now, is born of coveting. Lying is likewise, for many covet a situation that is contrary to the right, and are willing to lie about it.

Nothing could be more specific than this command:

Thou shalt not covet—

Thy neighbor's house, to defraud him of his property.

Thy neighbor's wife, to steal her in adultery and break up a home.

Nor his manservant nor his maidservant, thinking to deprive a neighbor of his helpers whom he needs.

Nor his ox, though it be better than your own.

Nor his ass, which might be a better worker than your own.

Nor anything that is thy neighbor's.

The command "Thou shalt not covet," if observed, would solve most of the world's ills today.

Chapter 20

THE GREAT COMMANDMENT

The Savior told the Jews in his day about the first and great commandment. It was a quotation from Moses, who in turn had received it from Jehovah originally. As expressed in Matthew, it reads:

But when the Pharisees had heard that he had put the Sadducees to silence, they were gathered together.

Then one of them, which was a lawyer, asked him a question, tempting him, and saying,

Master, which is the great commandment in the law?

Jesus said unto him, Thou shalt love the Lord thy God with all thy heart, and with all thy soul, and with all thy mind.

This is the first and great commandment.

And the second is like unto it, Thou shalt love thy neighbour as thyself.

On these two commandments hang all the law and the prophets. (Matthew 22:34-40.)

It was given as follows in Moses' day:

Hear, O Israel: The Lord our God is one Lord:

And thou shalt love the Lord thy God with all thine heart, and with all thy soul, and with all thy might.

And these words, which I command thee this day, shall be in thine heart:

And thou shalt teach them diligently unto thy children, and shalt talk of them when thou sittest in thine house, and when thou walkest by the way, and when thou liest down, and when thou risest up.

And thou shalt bind them for a sign upon thine hand, and they shall be as frontlets between thine eyes.

And thou shalt write them upon the posts of thy house, and on thy gates. (Deuteronomy 6:4-9.)

It was followed immediately by this forceful demand for obedience:

Then beware lest thou forget the Lord, which brought thee forth out of the land of Egypt, from the house of bondage.

Thou shalt fear the Lord thy God, and serve him, and shalt swear by his name.

Ye shall not go after other gods, of the gods of the people which are round about you;

(For the Lord thy God is a jealous God among you) lest the anger of the Lord thy God be kindled against thee, and destroy thee from off the face of the earth.

Ye shall not tempt the Lord your God, as ye tempted him in Massah.

Ye shall diligently keep the commandment of the Lord your God, and his testimonies, and his statutes, which he hath commanded thee.

And thou shalt do that which is right and good in the sight of the Lord: that it may be well with thee, and that thou mayest go in and possess the good land which the Lord sware unto thy fathers. (Deuteronomy 6:12-18.)

Often people ask why the Lord is so strict in his insistence upon complete obedience. Only such obedience will satisfy the terms of this first and great commandment.

As we consider it, we must always remember that it is inseparably connected with that other great charge given in the Sermon on the Mount: "Be ye therefore perfect, even as your Father which is in heaven is perfect." (Matthew 5:48.)

If we seek to emulate the life of Christ, we must concentrate on it with a great and sincere effort. If we hope to become like our Father in heaven, we must give it top priority in our lives.

Who can become a great musician or a great engineer or other highly skilled person without centering full attention on that objective?

But which is more difficult, to be a great musician or to become perfect like God?

We cannot reach perfection by imperfect means. Being lax in our attention to the Lord and slovenly in our obedience to him spell nothing but imperfection and failure.

The Lord knows this. Because he wants us to become like him, he requires that we follow his formula, and that requires consistent daily obedience, the living of his kind of life, the thinking of his kind of thoughts, in order that "the works that I do shall [ye] do also," and "greater works than these shall [ye] do." (John 14:12.)

Isn't that the way we attain perfection? If we do the works of God, we shall know of his doctrine, that it is true. (John 7:17.) If we do the works of God, we shall develop Christlike traits of character. We must change our ways, repent, leave our former worldliness, and follow him. But we must serve him with enthusiasm and not with slothfulness. There is a great lesson in this revelation:

> For behold, it is not meet that I should command in all things; for he that is compelled in all things, the same is a slothful and not a wise servant; wherefore he receiveth no reward.
> Verily I say, men should be anxiously engaged in a good cause, and do many things of their own free will, and bring to pass much righteousness;
> For the power is in them, wherein they are agents unto themselves. And inasmuch as men do good they shall in nowise lose their reward.
> But he that doeth not anything until he is commanded, and receiveth a commandment with doubtful heart, and keepeth it with slothfulness, the same is damned. (D&C 58:26-29.)

He speaks here of being slothful. Could it be that the Lord in creation made the sloth as a horrible example? He mentions slothfulness so often. Again he said:

> Wherefore, now let every man learn his duty, and to act in the office in which he is appointed, in all diligence.
> He that is slothful shall not be counted worthy to stand, and he that learns not his duty and shows himself not approved shall not be counted worthy to stand. (D&C 107:99-100.)

We shall always remember the instruction he gave to the Twelve in the days of Joseph Smith: ". . . I say unto all the Twelve: Arise and gird up your loins, take up your cross, follow me, and feed my sheep." (D&C 112:14.) Can half-hearted effort satisfy that charge?

What kind of lesson did the Lord teach Peter on the seashore when he commanded the fisherman to "feed my sheep"? (John 21:15-17.)

What did Paul have in mind when, near the end of his life, he wrote to Timothy and said, "I have fought a good fight, I have finished my course, I have kept the faith"? (2 Timothy 4:7.)

What did the Prophet Joseph Smith have in mind when he said, "I am going like a lamb to the slaughter, but I am calm as a summer's morning. I have a conscience void of offense toward God and toward all men." (*History of the Church* 6:555.)

In every instance it was dedication, complete dedication. It was a willingness to give even life itself to and for the work. Paul gave his life both in service and in martyrdom. Joseph Smith lived intensely and never measured the cost as he sought to use every hour and every minute in building the kingdom. Thus he gave a full life of service, but also like Paul, he finished his course in martyrdom.

When the Lord said, "O ye that embark in the service of God, see that ye serve him with all your heart, might, mind and strength" (D&C 4:2), that is what he meant: dedication, from each one for us.

Slothfulness and imperfection sow the seeds of failure and never can lift anyone "unto a perfect man, unto the measure of the stature of the fulness of Christ." (Ephesians 4:13.)

Love the Lord with all our hearts? Can we give him anything less? Serve him with all our might, mind, and strength? Can we turn a deaf ear to that?

And who would wish to give anything less if the facts were all understood?

We can become like him, but obedience to the gospel is the formula we must follow. There is no other way. That is why the Lord is strict with us. That is why we never can afford to serve him with hesitation or reservations. That is why we must say with Paul:

For I am not ashamed of the gospel of Christ: for it is the power of God unto salvation to every one that believeth; to the Jew first, and also to the Greek.

For therein is the righteousness of God revealed from faith to faith: as it is written, The just shall live by faith.

For the wrath of God is revealed from heaven against all ungodliness and unrighteousness of men, who hold the truth in unrighteousness. (Romans 1:16-18.)

In discussing this general theme President David O. McKay said:

Civilization has grown too complex for the human mind to visualize or to control. Unless man comes to a speedy realization that the higher and not the baser qualities of man must be developed, then the present status of civilization is in jeopardy. Life on the animal plane has as its ideal the survival of the fittest—kill or be killed, crush or be crushed, mangle or be mangled. For man, with his intelligence, this is a sure road to anguish and death.

The spiritual road has Christ as its goal. The individual lives for something higher than self. He hears the Savior's voice saying: "I am the way, the truth, and the life. . . ." (John 14:6.) Following that voice, he soon learns that there is no one great thing which he can do to attain happiness or eternal life. He learns that "life is made up not of great sacrifices or duties, but of little things in which smiles and kindness and small obligations given habitually are what win and preserve the heart and secure comfort." (*Gospel Ideals,* p. 388.)

While the laws of God are strict, and while he requires that we love and serve him with all our heart, might, mind, and strength, he also recognizes that we are mortal and that we do make mistakes. Therefore, he provides repentance.

Whereas he says that he hates the sin, he nevertheless loves us all because we are his children, and he earnestly hopes that we will develop to become like himself.

That is the purpose of the gospel. It helps us to overcome our weaknesses and rebuild our lives. That is the purpose of the atonement of Christ. That is why he gives us the opportunity of repentance and readjustment in our lives.

When John the Baptist began his work it was with the cry: "Repent ye: for the kingdom of heaven is at hand." (Matthew 3:2.) The same message was voiced by the Lord himself, who offered repentance, reconciliation, readjustment, and spiritual rehabilitation to all who would give ear to his words.

The reason for baptism was "for the remission of your sins." The entire purpose of the gospel is to help us overcome our evil ways, pattern our lives after the Lord's, and become like him.

That was the point in his commandment to become perfect even as our Father in heaven is perfect. Achieving perfection is overcoming weaknesses and building strengths within us.

Ezekiel was plain in this regard. Speaking for the Lord he said: "Have I any pleasure at all that the wicked should die? saith the Lord God: and not that he should return from his ways, and live?" (Ezekiel 18:23.)

He gives the assurance that if the wicked person repents, turns from his evil ways, and then "keeps all my statutes," he shall surely live, and "all his transgressions that he hath committed, they shall not be mentioned unto him: in his righteousness that he hath done he shall live." (Ezekiel 18:22.)

Of course he points to the opposite situation too, and explains that the unrepentant will be condemned, and "in his trespass that he hath trespassed, and in his sin that he hath sinned, in them shall he die." (Ezekiel 18:24.)

Explaining still further this principle of repentance, the Lord himself said this through Joseph Smith:

Therefore I command you to repent—repent, lest I smite you by the rod of my mouth, and by my wrath, and by my anger, and your sufferings be sore—how sore you know not, how exquisite you know not, yea, how hard to bear you know not.

For behold, I, God, have suffered these things for all, that they might not suffer if they would repent;

But if they would not repent they must suffer even as I;

Which suffering caused myself, even God, the greatest of all, to tremble because of pain, and to bleed at every pore, and to suffer both body and spirit—and would that I might not drink the bitter cup, and shrink—

Nevertheless, glory be to the Father, and I partook and finished my preparations unto the children of men. (D&C 19:15-19.)

Chapter 21

OTHER COMMANDMENTS

The commandments given the Israelites in Moses' day reached into every corner of their lives. They were taught indeed to perfect themselves, and become free from the sins, diseases, and conflicts of the other nations. Note a few examples.

Honesty

The Golden Rule is one of the greatest of Christian principles (Matthew 7:12), and inasmuch as the Savior gave the law to Moses (3 Nephi 15), it is not surprising to see so much said in it regarding honesty and doing to others as we would be done by. Said the Lord:

Ye shall not steal, neither deal falsely, neither lie one to another.

And ye shall not swear by my name falsely, neither shalt thou profane the name of thy God: I am the Lord.

Thou shalt not defraud thy neighbour, neither rob him: the wages of him that is hired shall not abide with thee all night until the morning.

Thou shalt not curse the deaf, nor put a stumblingblock before the blind, but shalt fear thy God: I am the Lord.

Ye shall do no unrighteousness in judgment: thou shalt not respect the person of the poor, nor honour the person of the mighty: but in righteousness shalt thou judge thy neighbour.

Thou shalt not go up and down as a talebearer among thy people: neither shalt thou stand against the blood of thy neighbour: I am the Lord.

Thou shalt not hate thy brother in thine heart: thou shalt in any wise rebuke thy neighbour, and not suffer sin upon him.

Thou shalt not avenge, nor bear any grudge against the children of thy people, but thou shalt love thy neighbour as thyself: I am the Lord. (Leviticus 19:11-18.)

This is specific also:

Thou shalt not have in thy bag divers weights, a great and a small.

Thou shalt not have in thine house divers measures, a great and a small.

But thou shalt have a perfect and just weight, a perfect and just measure shalt thou have: that thy days may be lengthened in the land which the Lord thy God giveth thee. (Deuteronomy 25:13-15.)

Repeatedly the Lord taught that "thou shalt not oppress a stranger" (Exodus 23:9 and Leviticus 19:33-34), but he was conscious also of the need to do a good turn to others. For example:

If thou meet thine enemy's ox or his ass going astray, thou shalt surely bring it back to him again.

If thou see the ass of him that hateth thee lying under his burden, and wouldest forbear to help him, thou shalt surely help with him.

Thou shalt not wrest the judgment of thy poor in his cause.

Keep thee far from a false matter; and the innocent and righteous slay thou not: for I will not justify the wicked. (Exodus 23:4-7.)

Moses also taught: "In all things that I have said unto you be circumspect." (Exodus 23:13.)

His protection of widows and orphans was almost fierce. Said he:

Ye shall not afflict any widow, or fatherless child.

If thou afflict them in any wise, and they cry at all unto me, I will surely hear their cry;

And my wrath shall wax hot, and I will kill you with the sword; and your wives shall be widows, and your children fatherless. (Exodus 22:22-24.)

Neither are we to take advantage of the poor, even in lending them money, for he said: "If thou lend money to any of my people that is poor by thee, thou shalt not be to him as an usurer, neither shalt thou lay upon him usury." (Exodus 22:25.)

And of the aged he said: "Thou shalt rise up before the hoary head, and honour the face of the old man, and fear thy God: I am the Lord." (Leviticus 19:32.)

Chastity

The Ten Commandments prohibit adultery. This commandment God has repeated over and over again. Virtue had high priority in the law. The homosexual, the adulterer, and the fornicator were all condemned of the Lord.

For example:

If a man be found lying with a woman married to an husband, then they shall both of them die, both the man that lay with the woman, and the woman: so shalt thou put away evil from Israel.

If a damsel that is a virgin be betrothed unto an husband, and a man find her in the city, and lie with her;

Then ye shall bring them both out unto the gate of that city, and ye shall stone them with stones that they die; the damsel, because she cried not, being in the city; and the man, because he hath humbled his neighbour's wife: so thou shalt put away evil from among you.

But if a man find a betrothed damsel in the field, and the man force her, and lie with her: then the man only that lay with her shall die:

But unto the damsel thou shalt do nothing; there is in the damsel no sin worthy of death: for as when a man riseth against his neighbour, and slayeth him, even so is this matter:

For he found her in the field, and the betrothed damsel cried, and there was none to save her.

If a man find a damsel that is a virgin, which is not betrothed, and lay hold on her, and lie with her, and they be found;

Then the man that lay with her shall give unto the damsel's father fifty shekels of silver, and she shall be his wife; because he hath humbled her, he may not put her away all his days.

A man shall not take his father's wife, nor discover his father's skirt. (Deuteronomy 22:22-30.)

In this same stern language the Lord gave this:

And the man that committeth adultery with another man's wife, even he that committeth adultery with his neighbour's wife, the adulterer and the adulteress shall surely be put to death.

And the man that lieth with his father's wife hath uncovered his father's nakedness: both of them shall surely be put to death; their blood shall be upon them.

And if a man lie with his daughter in law, both of them shall surely be put to death: they have wrought confusion; their blood shall be upon them.

If a man also lie with mankind, as he lieth with a woman, both of them have committed an abomination: they shall surely be put to death; their blood shall be upon them.

And if a man take a wife and her mother, it is wickedness; they shall be burnt with fire, both he and they; that there be no wickedness among you.

And if a man lie with a beast, he shall surely be put to death: and ye shall slay the beast.

And if a woman approach unto any beast, and lie down thereto, thou shalt kill the woman, and the beast: they shall surely be put to death; their blood shall be upon them.

And if a man shall take his sister, his father's daughter, or his mother's daughter, and see her nakedness, and she see his nakedness; it is a wicked thing; and they shall be cut off in the sight of their people: he hath uncovered his sister's nakedness; he shall bear his iniquity.

And if a man shall lie with a woman having her sickness, and shall uncover her nakedness; he hath discovered her fountain, and she hath uncovered the fountain of her blood: and both of them shall be cut off from among their people.

And thou shalt not uncover the nakedness of thy mother's sister, nor of thy father's sister: for he uncovereth his near kin: they shall bear their iniquity.

And if a man shall lie with his uncle's wife, he hath uncovered his uncle's nakedness: they shall bear their sin; they shall die childless.

And if a man shall take his brother's wife, it is an unclean thing: he hath uncovered his brother's nakedness; they shall be childless. (Leviticus 20:10-21.)

Verse 13 above relates to the homosexual, whose crime in that day merited death.

The command is repeated in Leviticus 18:22: "Thou shalt not lie with mankind, as with womankind: it is abomination."

This law was carried forward even to Paul's day, for he wrote the Romans:

For this cause God gave them up unto vile affections: for even their women did change the natural use into that which is against nature:

And likewise also the men, leaving the natural use of the woman, burned in their lust one toward another; men with men working that which is unseemly, and receiving in themselves that recompence of their error which was meet.

And even as they did not like to retain God in their knowledge, God gave them over to a reprobate mind, to do those things which are not convenient. (Romans 1:26-28.)

In this connection we should note: "There shall be no whore of the daughters of Israel, nor a sodomite of the sons of Israel." (Deuteronomy 23:17.)

The following may well be considered by young people who tempt each other: "And if a man entice a maid that is not betrothed, and lie with her, he shall surely endow her to be his wife. If her father utterly refuse to give her unto him, he shall pay money according to the dowry of virgins." (Exodus 22:16-17.)

Sex sin always has been one of the most reprehensible in the eyes of the Lord.

Obedience

In the day of Moses the Lord taught his people a lesson very much like that which evolved from the banishment of the Latter-day Saints from Jackson County, Missouri. The Prophet Joseph asked the Lord why the expulsion had taken place. The Lord answered:

I, the Lord, have suffered the affliction to come upon them, wherewith they have been afflicted, in consequence of their transgressions;

Yet I will own them, and they shall be mine in that day when I shall come to make up my jewels.

Therefore, they must needs be chastened and tried, even as Abraham, who was commanded to offer up his only son.

For all those who will not endure chastening, but deny me, cannot be sanctified.

Behold, I say unto you, there were jarrings, and contentions, and envyings, and strifes, and lustful and covetous desires among them; therefore by these things they polluted their inheritances.

They were slow to hearken unto the voice of the Lord their God; therefore, the Lord their God is slow to hearken unto their prayers, to answer them in the day of their trouble.

In the day of their peace they esteemed lightly my counsel; but, in the day of their trouble, of necessity they feel after me. (D&C 101:2-8.)

This same lesson was taught anciently, as we read in the first chapter of Deuteronomy. Because the people were disobedient, "The Lord would not hearken to [their] voice, nor give ear unto [them]." (Deuteronomy 1:37-45.)

And this he stressed:

When thou hast eaten and art full, then thou shalt bless the Lord thy God for the good land which he hath given thee.

Beware that thou forget not the Lord thy God, in not keeping his commandments, and his judgments, and his statutes, which I command thee this day:

Lest when thou hast eaten and art full, and hast built goodly houses, and dwelt therein;

And when thy herds and thy flocks multiply, and thy silver and thy gold is multiplied, and all that thou hast is multiplied;

Then thine heart be lifted up, and thou forget the Lord thy God, which brought thee forth out of the land of Egypt, from the house of bondage;

Who led thee through that great and terrible wilderness, wherein were fiery serpents, and scorpions, and drought, where there was no water; who brought thee forth water out of the rock of flint;

Who fed thee in the wilderness with manna, which thy fathers knew not, that he might humble thee, and that he might prove thee, to do thee good at thy latter end;

And thou say in thine heart, My power and the might of mine hand hath gotten me this wealth.

But thou shalt remember the Lord thy God: for it is he that giveth thee power to get wealth, that he may establish his covenant which he sware unto thy fathers, as it is this day.

And it shall be, if thou do at all forget the Lord thy God, and walk after other gods, and serve them, and worship them, I testify against you this day that ye shall surely perish.

As the nations which the Lord destroyeth before your face, so shall ye perish; because ye would not be obedient unto the voice of the Lord your God. (Deuteronomy 8:10-20.)

Marriage

The Lord was strict in requiring his people to marry within their own faith and their own race.

As the Israelites approached the Promised Land, knowing that it was then occupied by idolatrous nations, he declared:

Neither shalt thou make marriages with them; thy daughter thou shalt not give unto his son, nor his daughter shalt thou take unto thy son.

For they will turn away thy son from following me, that they may serve other gods: so will the anger of the Lord be kindled against you, and destroy thee suddenly. (Deuteronomy 7:3-4.)

He went so far as to say this also:

This is the thing which the Lord doth command concerning the daughters of Zelophehad, saying, Let them marry to whom they think best; only to the family of the tribe of their father shall they marry.

So shall not the inheritance of the children of Israel remove from tribe to tribe: for every one of the children of Israel shall keep himself to the inheritance of the tribe of his fathers.

And every daughter, that possesseth an inheritance in any tribe of the children of Israel, shall be wife unto one of the family of the tribe of her father, that the children of Israel may enjoy every man the inheritance of his fathers. (Numbers 36:6-8.)

It was most important that the faith be not diluted by intermarriages. It was all important that the faithful marry the faithful. This is also the advice of the leaders of today, who urge that we should marry in the faith and in the temple, which is the Lord's mode of marriage.

When we read revelations like section 131 of the Doctrine and Covenants, how can we think of doing otherwise? Thus similarly may we contemplate verses 15 to 17 in section 132 of that volume.

On the subject of intermarriages, President Spencer W. Kimball has said the following:

The Church of Jesus Christ of Latter-day Saints encourages with all its power and strength the marriage of its people within the Church and among the faithful in that church, and generally has found it to be wise to marry within the common customs, education, wealth, and tradition, and this because it fosters the backgrounds which have a great bearing upon the happiness of the couples.

We have found that it is still quite possible to live in different countries with different languages and culture and customs and still marry within one's own race and background.

We believe that it is wise for young people to usually seek out those of their own training, language, and background so that their new marriage has every possibility of developing into a happy marriage with a happy home and family, for marriage to us is the most sacred of all obligations, and we hope that every marriage is a successful one and a happy one. (Private correspondence in the author's file. Used by permission.)

It is interesting that the Lord insisted that a marriage should not be disturbed for one year even by war. Said he: "When a man hath taken a new wife, he shall not go out to war, neither shall he be charged with any business: but he shall be free at home one year, and shall cheer up his wife which he hath taken." (Deuteronomy 24:5.)

It is also of interest in this day to read: "The woman shall not wear that which pertaineth unto a man, neither shall a man put on a woman's garment: for all that do so are abomination unto the Lord thy God." (Deuteronomy 22:5.)

In cases of death this law was given:

If brethren dwell together, and one of them die, and have no child, the wife of the dead shall not marry without unto a stranger: her husband's brother shall go in unto her, and take her to him to wife, and perform the duty of an husband's brother unto her.

And it shall be, that the firstborn which she beareth shall succeed in the name of his brother which is dead, that his name be not put out of Israel.

And if the man like not to take his brother's wife, then let his brother's wife go up to the gate unto the elders, and say, My husband's brother refuseth to raise up unto his brother a name in Israel, he will not perform the duty of my husband's brother.

Then the elders of his city shall call him, and speak unto him: and if he stand to it, and say, I like not to take her;

Then shall his brother's wife come unto him in the presence of the elders, and loose his shoe from off his foot, and spit in his face, and shall answer and say, So shall it be done unto that man that will not build up his brother's house.

And his name shall be called in Israel, the house of him that hath his shoe loosed. (Deuteronomy 25:5-10.)

This was an old law going back into Genesis. It is noted in Genesis 38:8-11, as also in the story of Ruth, seen in the book of Ruth in the Bible. But of course this law is not applicable now.

Sin in Ignorance

Ignorance of the law was no excuse for disobedience to the law, and a penalty was required.

And if the whole congregation of Israel sin through ignorance, and the thing be hid from the eyes of the assembly, and they have done somewhat against any of the commandments of the Lord concerning things which should not be done, and are guilty;

And if any one of the common people sin through ignorance, while he doeth somewhat against any of the commandments of the Lord concerning things which ought not to be done, and be guilty;

Or if his sin, which he hath sinned, come to his knowledge: then he shall bring his offering, a kid of the goats, *a female without blemish,* for his sin which he hath sinned. (Leviticus 4:13, 27-28. Italics added.)

The Lord also said this:

If a soul commit a trespass, and sin through ignorance, in the holy things of the Lord; then he shall bring for his trespass unto the Lord a ram without blemish out of the flocks, with thy estimation by shekels of silver, after the shekel of the sanctuary, for a trespass offering:

And he shall make amends for the harm that he hath done in the holy thing, and shall add the fifth part thereto, and give it unto the priest: and the priest shall make an atonement for him with the ram of the trespass offering, and it shall be forgiven him. (Leviticus 5:15-16.)

Tithing

Tithing was an established principle among the Israelites. For example:

Thou shalt truly tithe all the increase of thy seed, that the field bringeth forth year by year.

And thou shalt eat before the Lord thy God, in the place which he shall choose to place his name there, the tithe of thy corn, of thy wine, and of thine oil, and the firstlings of thy herds and of thy flocks; that thou mayest learn to fear the Lord thy God always. (Deuteronomy 14:22-23.)

In Leviticus we read:

And all the tithe of the land, whether of the seed of the land, or of the fruit of the tree, is the Lord's: it is holy unto the Lord.

And if a man will at all redeem ought of his tithes, he shall add thereto the fifth part thereof.

And concerning the tithe of the herd, or of the flock, even of whatsoever passeth under the rod, the tenth shall be holy unto the Lord.

He shall not search whether it be good or bad, neither shall he change it: and if he change it at all, then both it and the change thereof shall be holy; it shall not be redeemed.

These are the commandments, which the Lord commanded Moses for the children of Israel in mount Sinai. (Leviticus 27:30-34.)

The law was handed down to the days of Malachi, who gave us this oft-quoted scripture:

> Will a man rob God? Yet ye have robbed me. But ye say, Wherein have we robbed thee? In tithes and offerings.
> Ye are cursed with a curse: for ye have robbed me, even this whole nation.
> Bring ye all the tithes into the storehouse, that there may be meat in mine house, and prove me now herewith, saith the Lord of hosts, if I will not open you the windows of heaven, and pour you out a blessing, that there shall not be room enough to receive it. (Malachi 3:8-10.)

Capital Punishment

With the present-day disputes over capital punishment, it is interesting to note that such punishment was common among the children of Israel for various types of sins from Sabbath breaking to adultery and murder.

Particularly in regard to murder we read:

> He that smiteth a man, so that he die, shall be surely put to death.
> And if a man lie not in wait, but God deliver him into his hand; then I will appoint thee a place whither he shall flee.
> But if a man come presumptuously upon his neighbour, to slay him with guile; thou shalt take him from mine altar, that he may die.
> And he that smiteth his father, or his mother, shall be surely put to death.
> And he that stealeth a man, and selleth him [as a slave], or if he be found in his hand, he shall surely be put to death.
> And he that curseth his father, or his mother, shall surely be put to death.
> And if men strive together, and one smite another with a stone, or with his fist, and he die not, but keepeth his bed:
> If he rise again, and walk abroad upon his staff, then shall he that smote him be quit: only he shall pay for the loss of his time, and shall cause him to be thoroughly healed.
> And if a man smite his servant, or his maid, with a rod, and he die under his hand; he shall be surely punished.
> Notwithstanding, if he continue a day or two, he shall not be punished: for he is his money.
> If men strive, and hurt a woman with child, so that her fruit depart from her, and yet no mischief follow: he shall be surely punished, according as the woman's husband will lay upon him; and he shall pay as the judges determine.
> And if any mischief follow, then thou shalt give life for life.
> Eye for eye, tooth for tooth, hand for hand, foot for foot.
> Burning for burning, wound for wound, stripe for stripe. (Exodus 21:12-25.)

Also in Deuteronomy we have:

But if any man hate his neighbour, and lie in wait for him, and rise up against him, and smite him mortally that he die, and fleeth into one of these cities:

Then the elders of his city shall send and fetch him thence, and deliver him into the hand of the avenger of blood, that he may die.

Thine eye shall not pity him, but thou shalt put away the guilt of innocent blood from Israel, that it may go well with thee. (Deuteronomy 19:11-13.)

Note particularly verse 13. The cry today is that it is inhuman to execute a murderer no matter how heinous the crime. Such advocates should read carefully what the Lord says about those condemned to die for murder: "Thine eye shall not pity him."

There was a responsibility to the community in these cases, as the Lord points out. The execution has as one purpose: "Thou shalt put away the guilt of innocent blood from Israel, that it may go well with thee."

In Leviticus we read: "And he that killeth any man shall surely be put to death. . . . And he that killeth a beast, he shall restore it: and he that killeth a man, he shall be put to death." (Leviticus 24:17, 21.)

In Numbers we read:

And if he smite him with an instrument of iron, so that he die, he is a murderer: the murderer shall surely be put to death.

And if he smite him with throwing a stone, wherewith he may die, and he die, he is a murderer: the murderer shall surely be put to death.

Or if he smite him with an hand weapon of wood, wherewith he may die, and he die, he is a murderer: the murderer shall surely be put to death.

The revenger of blood himself shall slay the murderer: when he meeteth him, he shall slay him.

But if he thrust him of hatred, or hurl at him by laying of wait, that he die;

Or in enmity smite him with his hand, that he die: he that smote him shall surely be put to death; for he is a murderer: the revenger of blood shall slay the murderer, when he meeteth him.

Whoso killeth any person, the murderer shall be put to death by the mouth of witnesses: but one witness shall not testify against any person to cause him to die.

Moreover ye shall take no satisfaction for the life of a murderer, which is guilty of death: but he shall be surely put to death. (Numbers 35:16-21, 30-31.)

Of course the Genesis pronouncement on this crime is well-known: "Whoso sheddeth man's blood, by man shall his blood be shed: for in the image of God made he man." (Genesis 9:6.)

Witchcraft

In all the generations, it seems that witchcraft or some other form of devil worship appears. It is known even today, with churches of devil worshipers actually being organized in some cities. There are also fortune tellers, "table lifters," and seances of one kind or another, all of which fall into the same general class. The Lord condemned all such.

Capital punishment was allotted to the witches of Moses' day: "Thou shalt not suffer a witch to live." (Exodus 22:18.)

In Leviticus we read: "Regard not them that have familiar spirits, neither seek after wizards, to be defiled by them: I am the Lord your God." (Leviticus 19:31.)

In that same book we have:

> And the soul that turneth after such as have familiar spirits, and after wizards, to go a whoring after them, I will even set my face against that soul, and will cut him off from among his people.
> A man also or woman that hath a familiar spirit, or that is a wizard, shall surely be put to death: they shall stone them with stones: their blood shall be upon them. (Leviticus 20:6, 27.)

It is interesting to read Paul's experience with the "possessed" girl who gave readings. (Acts 16:16.)

False Prophets

False prophets have been the bane of righteous people all through the ages. It was so in Moses' day; it is so in our day. In Deuteronomy the Lord warned against false prophets, "dreamers," and those who would give a sign or profess some wonderful thing. Said the Lord about them:

> Thou shalt not hearken unto the words of that prophet, or that dreamer of dreams: for the Lord your God proveth you, to know whether ye love the Lord your God with all your heart and with all your soul.
> Ye shall walk after the Lord your God, and fear him, and keep his commandments, and obey his voice, and ye shall serve him, and cleave unto him.
> *And that prophet, or that dreamer of dreams, shall be put to death; because he hath spoken to turn you away from the Lord your God,* which

brought you out of the land of Egypt, and redeemed you out of the house of bondage, to thrust thee out of the way which the Lord thy God commanded thee to walk in. So shalt thou put the evil away from the midst of thee. (Deuteronomy 13:1-5. Italics added.)

The Lord provided capital punishment for such as these, for he said:

If thy brother, the son of thy mother, or thy son, or thy daughter, or the wife of thy bosom, or thy friend, which is as thine own soul, entice thee secretly, saying, Let us go and serve other gods, which thou hast not known, thou, nor thy fathers;

Namely, of the gods of the people which are round about you, nigh unto thee, or far off from thee, from the one end of the earth even unto the other end of the earth;

Thou shalt not consent unto him, nor hearken unto him; neither shall thine eye pity him, neither shalt thou spare, neither shalt thou conceal him:

But thou shalt surely kill him; thine hand shall be first upon him to put him to death, and afterwards the hand of all the people.

And thou shalt stone him with stones, that he die; because he hath sought to thrust thee away from the Lord thy God, which brought thee out of the land of Egypt, from the house of bondage.

And all Israel shall hear, and fear, and shall do no more any such wickedness as this is among you. (Deuteronomy 13:6-11. Italics added.)

The Unclean

Moral uncleanness was abhorrent to the Lord, and he provided many methods of cleansing for guilty ones, as is indicated in his many commands against sex perversions.

He also opposed drinking alcoholic beverages, and made it a capital offense if anyone thus unclean came into the tabernacle. Then he laid down this principle: "That ye may put difference between holy and unholy, and between unclean and clean." (Leviticus 10:8-11.)

Eating Meat

Certain types of meat were forbidden to the Israelites as a matter of health, as is well-known, but the following is of particular interest:

When the Lord thy God shall enlarge thy border, as he hath promised thee, and thou shalt say, I will eat flesh, because thy soul longeth to eat flesh; thou mayest eat flesh, whatsoever thy soul lusteth after.

Only be sure that thou *eat not the blood:* for the blood is the life; and thou mayest not eat the life with the flesh. (Deuteronomy 12:20, 23.)

Mob Action

Mob activities have been distasteful and harmful all through the ages. Evidently there were some in Moses' day, for the Lord prohibited them. Said he: "Thou shalt not raise a false report: put not thine hand with the wicked to be an unrighteous witness. Thou shalt not follow a multitude to do evil; neither shalt thou speak in a case to decline after many to wrest judgment." (Exodus 23:1-2.)

President Joseph F. Smith said this about mobs:

One of the greatest menaces to our country is that of the combination of men into irresponsible, reckless mobs, wild with prejudice, hatred and fanaticism, led by men of ambition, or passion, or hatred. There is no other thing in the world that I can conceive of so absolutely obnoxious to God and good men as a combination of men and women filled with the spirit of mobocracy. Men combining together to stop or shut off the food supply from the mouth of the honest laborer to starve the man that is willing to work, and the wife and the children who are dependent upon him, because he is not willing to join a mob, is one of the most infamous perils and menaces to the people of our country today. I do not care who they are, or what name they go by. They are a menace to the peace of the world. (*Gospel Doctrine*, pp. 414-15.)

Be Ye Perfect

The command to be perfect as our Father in heaven is perfect has been with us for a long time. The Savior gave it in the Sermon on the Mount, and Paul expanded on it in his epistle to the Ephesians. (Ephesians 4.)

Moses gave it to his people as the great objective to be gained, and his law was: "Thou shalt be perfect with the Lord thy God." (Deuteronomy 18:13.)

Many are the other laws. Only these few suggestions are given here. But as the laws are studied, it is easily seen that they make a marvelous "schoolmaster" to lead one to Christ.

Chapter 22

THE PENTATEUCH

Moses did write the first part of the Bible, and what he wrote is scripture in the most real sense of the word.

For years the so-called higher critics have assailed his authorship, some saying that he may have written one or two of those books, with others disavowing his authorship altogether.

One of their objections is to an occasional change in style of writing. Another is his use of the titles *Jehovah* and *God*. Still another says that Moses could not possibly have recorded the account of his own death. (Deuteronomy 34; Joshua 1:1-2.)

It will be remembered that the first Nephi of the Book of Mormon obtained the brass plates of Laban, thus providing an invaluable record for the use of the Nephites. His father Lehi read those plates. The record says:

> And after they had given thanks unto the God of Israel, my father, Lehi, took the records which were engraven upon the plates of brass, and he did search them from the beginning.
>
> And he beheld that *they did contain the five books of Moses*, which gave an account of the creation of the world, and also of Adam and Eve, who were our first parents;
>
> And also a record of the Jews from the beginning, even down to the commencement of the reign of Zedekiah, king of Judah;
>
> And also the prophecies of the holy prophets, from the beginning, even down to the commencement of the reign of Zedekiah; and also many prophecies which have been spoken by the mouth of Jeremiah.
>
> And it came to pass that my father, Lehi, also found upon the plates of brass a genealogy of his fathers; wherefore he knew that he was a descendant of Joseph; yea, even that Joseph who was the son of Jacob, who was sold into Egypt, and who was preserved by the hand of the Lord, that he might preserve his father, Jacob, and all his household from perishing with famine.
>
> And they were also led out of captivity and out of the land of Egypt, by the same God who had preserved them.
>
> And thus my father, Lehi, did discover the genealogy of his fathers. And Laban also was a descendant of Joseph, wherefore he and his fathers had kept the records.

And now when my father saw all these things, he was filled with the Spirit, and began to prophesy concerning his seed—

That these plates of brass should go forth unto all nations, kindreds, tongues, and people who were of his seed.

Wherefore, he said that these plates of brass should never perish; neither should they be dimmed any more by time. And he prophesied many things concerning his seed. (1 Nephi 5:10-19.)

Would he have called them the five books of Moses if they were not the books of Moses?

Nephi also had access to the writings of Moses, for he said:

And I did read many things unto them which were written in the book of Moses; but that I might more fully persuade them to believe in the Lord their Redeemer I did read unto them that which was written by the prophet Isaiah; for I did liken all scriptures unto us, that it might be for our profit and learning. (1 Nephi 19:23.)

Nephi gave this testimony concerning the writings of Moses:

And the Lord will surely prepare a way for his people, unto the fulfilling of the words of Moses, which he spake, saying: A prophet shall the Lord your God raise up unto you, like unto me; him shall ye hear in all things whatsoever he shall say unto you. And it shall come to pass that all those who will not hear that prophet shall be cut off from among the people.

And now I, Nephi, declare unto you, that this prophet of whom Moses spake was the Holy One of Israel; wherefore, he shall execute judgment in righteousness. (1 Nephi 22:20-21.)

Here is another evidence that Moses testified of Christ. And by what means did he give that testimony? In his writings!

And how did Nephi have access to Moses' testimony? In Moses' writings, recorded on the brass plates!

In the book of Helaman as well as elsewhere in the Book of Mormon, reference is made to the crossing of the Israelites through the Red Sea when they "came through upon dry ground." (Helaman 8:11.)

Verse 16 of this chapter is notable: "And now behold, Moses did not only testify of these things, but also all the holy prophets, from his days even to the days of Abraham."

And then note what he said:

Yea, and behold, Abraham saw of his coming, and was filled with gladness and did rejoice.

Yea, and behold I say unto you, that Abraham not only knew of these things, but there were many before the days of Abraham who were called by the order of God; yea, even after the order of his Son; and this that it should be shown unto the people, a great many thousand years before his coming, that even redemption should come unto them.

And now I would that ye should know, that even since the days of Abraham there have been many prophets that have testified these things; yea, behold, the prophet Zenos did testify boldly; for the which he was slain.

And behold, also Zenock, and also Ezias, and also Isaiah, and Jeremiah, (Jeremiah being that same prophet who testified of the destruction of Jerusalem) and now we know that Jerusalem was destroyed according to the words of Jeremiah. O then why not the Son of God come, according to his prophecy? (Helaman 8:17-20.)

Where would ancient American prophets have learned about that episode in Abraham's life if not from the books of Moses on the brass plates?

Likewise they knew much else of Abraham, Isaac, and Jacob, and of Melchizedek, the great king of Salem. (Alma 13 and Helaman 8.) Where would they have learned of these men and the details of their activities?

Again it was from the brass plates, which recorded the books of Moses and which were read and used and apparently published among the Nephites for centuries. (Alma 14:8; 18:36; 22:12; 33:14; 37:3.)

During his stay among the Nephites the Savior spoke of the fulfillment of Moses' words. Where would the Nephites have learned of those words? Obviously they knew of them, for the Savior spoke of them rather intimately.

Again their source was Moses' work written on the brass plates and republished among them.

No one can note the importance that Lehi placed on those plates without realizing that they were intended to be a guide to the Nephites down through all their generations. (3 Nephi 15; 3 Nephi 20:23; 3 Nephi 21:11.)

So again the Book of Mormon sustains the Bible and affirms that Moses did write extensively, most likely far more than what we have in our present Pentateuch.

Chapter 23

MOSES AND CHRIST

The Book of Mormon and the Bible stand as joint witnesses for both Christ the Savior and Moses his prophet.

As Jesus testified of Moses, so likewise did Moses testify of Christ, although much of his testimony is not in our present-day Bible. But obviously it was in the scriptures available to the people of Jesus' day.

It is faith-promoting indeed to note how consistent the various books of scripture are, one with another; how the revelations in the various ages all harmonize; and how the words of the prophets, no matter when or where they lived, testify of our Savior, Jesus Christ.

When critics attacked him, the Lord responded by saying to them: "Search the scriptures; for in them ye think ye have eternal life; and *they are they which testify of me.*" (John 5:39. Italics added.)

He never would have said that if the scriptures available to the people of that day did not testify of him. He urged them to read the scriptures that they might see how the prophets whom they adored, but now long since dead, actually did foretell his coming. They testified of him—the Savior. And Moses was one of them.

As the Savior elaborated on this point he said:

I am come in my Father's name, and ye receive me not: if another shall come in his own name, him ye will receive.

How can ye believe, which receive honour one of another, and seek not the honour that cometh from God only?

Do not think that I will accuse you to the Father: there is one that accuseth you, even Moses, in whom ye trust.

For had ye believed Moses, ye would have believed me: *for he wrote of me.*

But if ye believe not his writings, how shall ye believe my words? (John 5:43-47. Italics added.)

The conversation the Lord had with the two disciples en route to Emmaus, following the resurrection, is well remembered by all Bible readers.

As the disciples approached the village, "they talked together of all these things which had happened. And it came to pass, that, while they communed together and reasoned, Jesus himself drew near, and went with them." (Luke 24:14-15.)

They told the resurrected Savior, whom they as yet did not recognize, of the events pertaining to the crucifixion. They then explained about the empty sepulchre and the angels stationed at the door "which said that he was alive." They related also that some of the disciples had likewise seen the forsaken burial place, "but him they saw not." Then the Lord, still unrecognized, spoke to them and said:

"O fools, and slow of heart to believe all that the prophets have spoken:

"Ought not Christ to have suffered these things, and to enter into his glory?

"*And beginning at Moses and all the prophets,* he expounded unto them *in all the scriptures* the things concerning himself." (Luke 24:25-27. Italics added.)

Note that the Lord quoted both Moses and the other prophets expounding "in all the scriptures the things *concerning himself.*"

This is another evidence of the incompleteness of our present-day Bible, but it likewise gives evidence that the ancients had the fuller, more complete scriptures, even though they were not all handed down to us.

Peter's address in the third chapter of Acts is enlightening on this point.

While Paul was in Rome he likewise used the scriptures to testify of Jesus. Would he not have used those also quoted by the Savior? The scripture says: "And Paul dwelt two whole years in his own hired house, and received all that came in unto him, Preaching the kingdom of God, and teaching those things which concern the Lord Jesus Christ, with all confidence, no man forbidding him." (Acts 28:30-31.)

Paul also wrote:

Paul, a servant of Jesus Christ, called to be an apostle, separated unto
the gospel of God, *Which he had promised afore by his prophets in the holy
scriptures,*
Concerning his Son Jesus Christ our Lord, which was made of the
seed of David according to the flesh;
And declared to be the Son of God with power, according to the
spirit of holiness, by the resurrection from the dead:
By whom we have received grace and apostleship, for obedience to
the faith among all nations, for his name:
Among whom are ye also the called of Jesus Christ. (Romans 1:1-6.
Italics added.)

One of the most interesting passages indicating that
Moses testified of Christ is that in which we read of Philip
bringing Nathanael to visit the Lord. It will be remembered
that it was this same Nathanael who said, "Can any good
thing come out of Nazareth?"

The day following Jesus would go forth into Galilee, and findeth
Philip, and saith unto him, Follow me.
Now Philip was of Bethsaida, the city of Andrew and Peter.
Philip findeth Nathanael, and saith unto him, We have found him, *of
whom Moses in the law, and the prophets, did write, Jesus of Nazareth,* the
son of Joseph.
And Nathanael said unto him, Can there any good thing come out of
Nazareth? Philip saith unto him, Come and see.
Jesus saw Nathanael coming to him, and saith of him, Behold an Is-
raelite indeed, in whom is no guile!
Nathanael saith unto him, Whence knowest thou me? Jesus answered
and said unto him, Before that Philip called thee, when thou wast under
the fig tree, I saw thee.
Nathanael answered and saith unto him, Rabbi, thou art the Son of
God; thou art the King of Israel. (John 1:43-49. Italics added.)

When Peter went to Cornelius, he again spoke of Christ,
but would he have failed to use Moses' testimony, since
Moses was regarded as the one great authority among the
people of that day? Said Peter: *"To him give all the prophets
witness,* that through his name whosoever believeth in him
shall receive remission of sins." (Acts 10:43. Italics added.)

One of the most remarkable and faith-promoting portions of the Book of Mormon is the account of Abinadi's appearance before the wicked King Noah and his equally evil
priests. Not only does Abinadi reveal that Moses spoke of
Christ, but he gives a most enlightening portrayal of the rela-

tionship of the law of Moses to the gospel. This relationship is vital to our understanding.

And moreover, I say unto you, that salvation doth not come by the law alone; and were it not for the atonement, which God himself shall make for the sins and iniquities of his people, that they must unavoidably perish, notwithstanding the law of Moses.

And now I say unto you that it was expedient that there should be a law given to the children of Israel, yea, even a very strict law; for they were a stiffnecked people, quick to do iniquity, and slow to remember the Lord their God;

Therefore there was a law given them, yea, a law of performances and of ordinances, a law which they were to observe strictly from day to day, to keep them in remembrance of God and their duty towards him.

But behold, I say unto you, that all these things were types of things to come.

And now, did they understand the law? I say unto you, Nay, they did not all understand the law; and this because of the hardness of their hearts; for they understood not that there could not any man be saved except it were through the redemption of God.

For behold, *did not Moses prophesy unto them concerning the coming of the Messiah,* and that God should redeem his people? *Yea, and even all the prophets who have prophesied ever since the world began*—have they not spoken more or less concerning these things?

Have they not said that God himself should come down among the children of men, and take upon him the form of man, and go forth in mighty power upon the face of the earth?

Yea, and have they not said also that he should bring to pass the resurrection of the dead, and that he, himself, should be oppressed and afflicted? (Mosiah 13:28-35. Italics added.)

Again we see how the Bible and the Book of Mormon are indeed as "one in thine hand." (Ezekiel 37:17.)

It was Paul who explained to the Galatians that the law of Moses was merely a "schoolmaster" to bring the wayward Israelites back to the gospel. (Galatians 3:24-29.) Could it bring them back to Christ if the people were not told of Christ?

It was the Savior who gave the law to Moses, as we read in 3 Nephi 15:4-10.

The ancients before Moses had the gospel, including such men as Enoch, Melchizedek, Abraham, Isaac and Jacob, Jared of the Book of Mormon, and his brother and their families of the time of the tower of Babel.

The apostle Paul taught:

Know ye therefore that they which are of faith, the same are the children of Abraham.

And the scripture, foreseeing that God would justify the heathen
through faith, *preached before the gospel unto Abraham,* saying, In thee
shall all nations be blessed.
So then they which be of faith are blessed with faithful Abraham.
(Galatians 3:7-9. Italics added.)

When Paul spoke of the ancients in his letter to the Hebrews, he said: "For unto us was the gospel preached, as well
as unto them: but the word preached did not profit them, not
being mixed with faith in them that heard it." (Hebrews 4:2.)

And there is much significance also to this:

Moreover, brethren, I would not that ye should be ignorant, how that
all our fathers were under the cloud, and all passed through the sea;
And were all baptized unto Moses in the cloud and in the sea;
And did all eat the same spiritual meat;
And did all drink the same spiritual drink: for they drank of that
spiritual Rock that followed them: and that Rock was Christ. (1 Corinthians 10:1-4.)

The Prophet Joseph Smith made an interesting comment
at one time concerning Abel and his understanding of the
gospel. Said the Prophet:

It is said by Paul in his letter to the Hebrew brethren, that Abel obtained witness that he was righteous, God testifying of his gifts. To whom
did God testify of the gifts of Abel, was it to Paul? We have very little on
this important subject in the forepart of the Bible. But it is said that Abel
himself obtained witness that he was righteous.
Then certainly God spoke to him: indeed, it is said that God talked
with him; and if He did, would He not, seeing that Abel was righteous deliver to him the whole plan of the Gospel? And is not the Gospel the news
of the redemption?
How could Abel offer a sacrifice and look forward with faith on the
Son of God for a remission of his sins, and not understand the Gospel?
The mere shedding of the blood of beasts or offering anything else in
sacrifice, could not procure a remission of sins, except it were performed
in faith of something to come; if it could, Cain's offering must have been
as good as Abel's.
And if Abel was taught of the coming of the Son of God, was he not
taught also of His ordinances? We all admit that the Gospel has ordinances, and if so, had it not always ordinances, and were not its ordinances always the same? (*Teachings of the Prophet Joseph Smith,* p. 59.)

The Pearl of Great Price teaches that Adam was baptized
according to the rules of the gospel (Moses 6:64) and was
commanded to teach the gospel to his children (Moses 6:51-
58).

Christ was well known to the Book of Mormon prophets and appeared to some of them. Revelation was given to them in which Jesus Christ clearly identified himself, as for example when he spoke to Alma:

Thou art my servant; and I covenant with thee that thou shalt have eternal life; and thou shalt serve me and go forth in my name, and shalt gather together my sheep.

And he that will hear my voice shall be my sheep; and him shall ye receive into the church, and him will I also receive.

For behold, this is my church; whosoever is baptized shall be baptized unto repentance. And whomsoever ye receive shall believe in my name; and him will I freely forgive.

For it is I that taketh upon me the sins of the world; for it is I that hath created them; and it is I that granteth unto him that believeth unto the end a place at my right hand.

For behold, in my name are they called; and if they know me they shall come forth, and shall have a place eternally at my right hand.

And it shall come to pass that when the second trump shall sound then shall they that never knew me come forth and shall stand before me.

And then shall they know that I am the Lord their God, that I am their Redeemer; but they would not be redeemed.

And then I will confess unto them that I never knew them; and they shall depart into everlasting fire prepared for the devil and his angels.

Therefore I say unto you, that he that will not hear my voice, the same shall ye not receive into my church, for him I will not receive at the last day. (Mosiah 26:20-28.)

This occurred a century before the mortal birth of Jesus.

The Israelites lost much of their faith during their Egyptian bondage. Of necessity they had to be brought back to Christ by some schoolmaster, and the law of Moses was that instrument.

In all of this, Christ dealt with Moses, and Moses dealt with Christ (Jehovah of the Old Testament). The two were closely and intimately associated. The existence of Christ, the existence of the law, and the manner in which the gospel was brought back by the mortal ministry of the Savior all testify to the reality of Moses' existence and the importance of his mission.

As Christ lived, so did Moses live. As Moses was a great prophet of God, so he testified of his Lord and Master, and ours.

Chapter 24

MOSES AND CREATION

Moses had two missions. One was to rescue Israel from Egyptian bondage, restoring the nation to the Land of Promise. The other was to convert the tribes to the worship of the true God. In both of these missions he was constantly taught and directed by the Almighty himself; he had such a close relationship with the Lord that it even approached being a companionship.

Abraham had been called the friend of God. Moses was all of that and more. Whereas Abraham was the progenitor of the Israelites, Moses was their great teacher and liberator.

Moses knew God from close relationship. One portion of his experience is detailed in the first chapter of the Book of Moses.

What a call it was that came to Moses, and what mighty revelations!

And calling upon the name of God, he beheld his glory again, for it was upon him; and he heard a voice, saying: Blessed art thou, Moses, for I, the Almighty, have chosen thee, and thou shalt be made stronger than many waters; for they shall obey thy command as if thou wert God.

And lo, I am with thee, even unto the end of thy days; for thou shalt deliver my people from bondage, even Israel my chosen.

And it came to pass, as the voice was still speaking, Moses cast his eyes and beheld the earth, yea, even all of it; and there was not a particle of it which he did not behold, discerning it by the spirit of God.

And he beheld also the inhabitants thereof, and there was not a soul which he beheld not; and he discerned them by the Spirit of God; and their numbers were great, even numberless as the sand upon the sea shore.

And he beheld many lands; and each land was called earth, and there were inhabitants on the face thereof.

And it came to pass that Moses called upon God, saying: Tell me, I pray thee, why these things are so, and by what thou madest them?

And behold, the glory of the Lord was upon Moses, so that Moses stood in the presence of God, and talked with him face to face. And the Lord God said unto Moses: For mine own purpose have I made these things. Here is wisdom and it remaineth in me.

And by the Word of my power, have I created them, which is mine Only Begotten Son, who is full of grace and truth.

And worlds without number have I created; and I also created them for mine own purpose; and by the Son I created them, which is mine Only Begotten.

And the first man of all men have I called Adam, which is many.

But only an account of this earth, and the inhabitants thereof, give I unto you. For behold, there are many worlds that have passed away by the Word of my power. And there are many that now stand, and innumerable are they unto man; but all things are numbered unto me, for they are mine and I know them.

And it came to pass that Moses spake unto the Lord, saying: Be merciful unto thy servant, O God, and tell me concerning this earth, and the inhabitants thereof, and also the heavens, and then thy servant will be content.

And the Lord God spake unto Moses, saying: The heavens, they are many, and they cannot be numbered unto man; but they are numbered unto me, for they are mine.

And as one earth shall pass away, and the heavens thereof even so shall another come; and there is no end to my works, neither to my words.

For behold, this is my work and my glory—to bring to pass the immortality and eternal life of man.

And now, Moses, my son, I will speak unto thee concerning this earth upon which thou standest; and thou shalt write the things which I shall speak.

And in a day when the children of men shall esteem my words as naught and take many of them from the book which thou shalt write, behold, I will raise up another like unto thee; and they shall be had again among the children of men—among as many as shall believe.

(These words were spoken unto Moses in the mount, the name of which shall not be known among the children of men. And now they are spoken unto you. Show them not unto any except them that believe. Even so. Amen.) (Moses 1:25-42.)

One of the most illuminating, comforting, and faith-building portions of all the revelations to Moses is that which describes the primeval council in heaven—how the Savior was appointed and how Satan chose his rebellious role. This alone gives us a widely expanded view of the gospel and its purpose. (Moses 4:1-4.)

Also in these writings is direct revelation giving us the assurance that man truly is made in the image and likeness of God by reason of the fact that God is our Father and we are his children.

Was God alone in the creation? The revelation to Moses shows that the Father and the Son acted jointly in the work of creation. For example, the Lord spoke to Moses and said:

"And I, God, said unto mine Only Begotten, which was with me from the beginning: Let us make man in our image, after our likeness; and it was so." (Moses 2:26.)

Many scholars have puzzled over the use of the plural form in Genesis as they have read: "And God said, Let *us* make man in *our* image, after *our* likeness." (Genesis 1:26. Italics added.) The Book of Moses explains fully, and the Book of Abraham confirms it.

It is remarkable that "the glory of the Lord was upon Moses, so that Moses stood in the presence of God, and talked with him face to face." (Moses 1:31.) How few, even of the prophets, have enjoyed such a blessing!

The Lord by revelation told Moses the story of creation, with what is now the beginning of the book of Genesis, and which constitutes chapters two through four of the Book of Moses.

The Lord prepared Moses for this description of creation by telling him of the extent of it, far beyond our universe. (Moses 1:31-41.)

Those who challenge Genesis, as well as Moses personally, fail to recognize the great factor of revelation. Obviously the Lord desired that his people here on earth—all of us his children—should know about our origin and learn that the earth was made for us. And he desired to have us know that we, as immortal spirits clothed in physical bodies, are his spirit children, even as he revealed it to the apostle Paul (Acts 17:28-29), and that his work and glory are to bring about the immortality and eternal life of man (Moses 1:39).

This could only have been given by revelation, and that revelation came to the prophets, Moses being one of them.

Creation came, but not by accident; life came, but not spontaneously. Both came by act of God himself, as a step toward helping us to become like him. It is only natural for children to become like their parents, and we are his offspring.

Not only did the Lord reveal these great truths to Moses, but likewise he told him the history of the earth from the creation to the flood, all of which is recorded in the Book of Moses.

Some of the critics who discount the writings pertaining to the periods both before and after the flood ask, How could anyone know? And what is the answer?

"And these are the words which I spake unto my servant Moses, and they are true even as I will; and I have spoken them unto you [Joseph Smith]." (Moses 4:32.)

And also: "These words were spoken unto Moses in the mount, the name of which shall not be known among the children of men. And now they are spoken unto you [Joseph Smith]." (Moses 1:42.)

How did Moses know? By revelation!

Chapter 25

GENESIS— THE BEGINNING

How did it all begin, this earth and all life upon it? Who can tell the facts in the drama that gave each of us life?

It was Moses who wrote the account we have in the book of Genesis, but what is there seems to be a shortened version of his original text.

What appears in the Pearl of Great Price as the Book of Moses is an accurate and more detailed record of what he wrote. This we know by the revelations given to Joseph Smith.

The Book of Abraham, also in the Pearl of Great Price, provides much of tremendous interest concerning the creation and the manner of it, revealing the close association of "the Gods" in making the earth and providing life upon it. Moses shows "the Gods" to be the Father and the Son. (Moses 2:26.)

In revelation to our modern prophet, the Lord repeated what was said to Moses:

VISIONS OF MOSES *as revealed to Joseph Smith in June, 1830.*
The words of God, which he spake unto Moses at a time when Moses was caught up into an exceedingly high mountain,
And he saw God face to face, and he talked with him, and the glory of God was upon Moses; therefore Moses could endure his presence.
And God spake unto Moses, saying: Behold, I am the Lord God Almighty, and Endless is my name; for I am without beginning of days or end of years; and is not this endless?
And, behold, thou art my son; wherefore look, and I will show thee the workmanship of mine hands; but not all, for my works are without end.... (Moses 1:1-4)

And then the sacred record begins the account of creation:

And it came to pass that the Lord spake unto Moses, saying: Behold, I reveal unto you concerning this heaven, and this earth; *write the words which I speak.* I am the Beginning and the End, the Almighty God; by mine Only Begotten I created these things; yea, in the beginning I created the heaven, and the earth upon which thou standest.

And the earth was without form, and void; and I caused darkness to come up upon the face of the deep; and my Spirit moved upon the face of the water; for I am God.

And I, God, said: Let there be light; and there was light. (Moses 2:1-3. Italics added.)

It is interesting to compare Moses' treatise with that of Abraham, to whom the story of creation was revealed also. Abraham recorded it in slightly different words but the facts are identical:

And then the Lord said: Let us go down. And they went down at the beginning, and they, that is the Gods, organized and formed the heavens and the earth.

And the earth, after it was formed, was empty and desolate, because they had not formed anything but the earth; and darkness reigned upon the face of the deep, and the Spirit of the Gods was brooding upon the face of the waters.

And they (the Gods) said: Let there be light; and there was light. (Abraham 4:1-3.)

The Bible version, of course, simply reads: "In the beginning God created the heaven and the earth" (Genesis 1:1), and so he did!

The earth did not come into being by some spontaneous but unknown means, as the scholars say. It was ordered and planned by the Almighty himself, even before the creation was begun. When the primeval council was held in heaven; when Jehovah was chosen as the Savior, and Satan rebelled; when all the sons of God shouted for joy—in that period was it planned, designed, and ordered. (Moses 4:1-3; Job 38.)

Since we have the certainty of the special divine creation, and since we have it on God's own word by revelation, there is no room for speculation on this point in the minds of the devout. We are not bound by any man-devised hypothesis. Research is commendable, but it has never factually explained the origin either of the earth or of life on the earth. It has produced theories and deductions, but never the actual truth about our origin.

Revelation has given us the facts. God made the earth, but not "out of nothing," as the sectarians dogmatize. He took existing materials, as the scripture notes, and organized

them into the earth. (Abraham 3:24; 4:1.) He did so for a
particular purpose: to provide a mortal home for us, his
spirit offspring who were with him in the preexistence, and
who comprised the hosts of heaven who shouted for joy, as
referred to in Job 38.

A. Cressy Morrison, science writer, regarded Genesis as
the most correct although the briefest account of creation
ever written, and added that its detail is not changed by any
information subsequently discovered by modern men.

Morrison, recently deceased, was president of the New
York Academy of Sciences and the American Institute of the
City of New York; a member of the executive board of the
National Research Council; a fellow of the American
Museum of Natural History; and a life member of the Royal
Institution of Great Britain.

His little book *Man Does Not Stand Alone* is priceless
reading for the average inquiring mind. Its final chapter
begins:

> The first chapter of Genesis contains the real story of creation and its
> essence has not been changed by knowledge acquired since it was written.
> This statement will cause a smile to develop on the genial face of the
> scientist and a look of incredulity but satisfaction from the true believer.
> The differences have arisen over details which are not worth controversy.
> (Old Tappan, New Jersey: Fleming H. Revell Co., 1946, p. 101.)

Genesis says there were six creative periods or "days" of
unknown length, and that certain steps in creation char-
acterized each "day." Morrison says science agrees.

Genesis says that all forms of life were commanded to
reproduce themselves, but always and only "after their
kind." Science agrees that all forms of life do bring forth
only after their own kind.

For example, Theodosius Dobzhansky, in his *Mankind
Evolving,* says: "Genetically effective interbreeding is absent
between species. Contemporaneous species do not exchange
genes, or do so but rarely. There is, for example, no living
species with which man could interbreed. Although the
horse and donkey species are hybridized on a large scale to
produce mules, the mules are wholly or almost wholly sterile
so that no gene interchange results." (London: Yale
University Press, 1962, pp. 183-84.)

Professor T. H. Morgan of the California Institute of Technology writes: "Within the period of human history we do not find a single instance of the transformation of one species into another one. It may be claimed then that the theory of descent is lacking in the most essential feature that it takes to place it on a scientific basis." (Hand, *Why I Accept the Genesis Record,* p. 27.)

A Britisher, Dr. McNair Wilson, editor of the Oxford Medical Publications, wrote: "An increase of knowledge about biology has tended to emphasize the extreme rigidity of type and, more and more, to discount the idea of transmutation from one type to another—the essential basis of Darwinism." (Ibid., p. 49.)

The September 1976 issue of *National Geographic* carried an extensive dissertation on the development of a single cell and the stability of the species, as revealed by the "new biology."

The discussion points out that biologists have found that every cell contains the "entire repertoire" of genes for any given plant or animal; that "each cell is brimming with as many as two hundred trillion tiny groups of atoms"; yet when reproduction comes, each makes exact copies of itself. Could an accident produce all this?

"Each gene," the author says, "or distinct segment of the long DNA strand, contains instructions for making *one specific* protein."

Reproduction of sponges, for example, is illustrated. Each new sponge is an organism exactly like the original. "Interestingly, when you put cells from two different sponges together, each will recognize its own. . . . One of the primal needs of an organism is to recognize its own cells," the writer goes on.

Speaking of the chromosomes he says:

Each chromosome is a package of DNA divided into hundreds of different genes. It is from the chromosomes that the genes send messages to other parts of the cell on how to make the enzymes and other proteins in which that cell specializes.

The genes responsible for blue eyes or any other physical trait are always located as *specific* spots on *specific* chromosomes. Our 46 chromosome "threads" linked together would measure more than six feet. Yet the nucleus that contains them is less than four ten-thousandths of an inch in diameter. The nucleus is most dynamic when a cell divides. Before division, the DNA in each chromosome *duplicates.* The result is two *identical* sets of chromosomes. (Rick Gore, "The Awesome Worlds Within a Cell," *National Geographic,* September 1976, pp. 355-95. Italics added.)

An interesting discussion on the impossibility of interbreeding the species is provided by another Britisher, Henry R. Kindersley, who speaks of the hare and the rabbit, animals which look alike to most people. Yet, he says, "examined as living species we find that the hare and the rabbit absolutely refuse to interbreed. Moreover one of them produces its young blind and naked and the other open-eyed and covered with fur." (*The Bible and Evolution, Evidence of History and Science,* 64:195-96.)

One of the most vital facts in the entire creation story is the account of the formation of man. When God spoke of making man in his image he spoke of *mankind*—male and female, not just of an isolated person or even a single couple as Adam and Eve. He thereby provided mortal life for us all.

And I, God, said unto mine Only Begotten, which was with me from the beginning: Let us make man in our image, after our likeness; and it was so. And I, God, said: Let them have dominion over the fishes of the sea, and over the fowl of the air, and over the cattle, and over all the earth, and over every creeping thing that creepeth upon the earth.

And I, God, created man in mine own image, in the image of mine Only Begotten created I him; male and female created I them.

And I, God, blessed them, and said unto them: Be fruitful, and multiply, and replenish the earth, and subdue it, and have dominion over the fish of the sea, and over the fowl of the air, and over every living thing that moveth upon the earth.

And I, God, said unto man: Behold, I have given you every herb bearing seed, which is upon the face of all the earth, and every tree in the which shall be the fruit of a tree yielding seed; to you it shall be for meat.

And to every beast of the earth, and to every fowl of the air, and to everything that creepeth upon the earth, wherein I grant life, there shall be given every clean herb for meat; and it was so, even as I spake.

And I, God, saw everything that I had made, and, behold, all things which I had made were very good; and the evening and the morning were the sixth day. (Moses 2:26-31.)

He commanded them to reproduce themselves. They too would bring forth only "after their kind." It could be in no other way. Each form of life was destined to bring forth after its own kind so that it would be perpetuated in the earth and avoid confusion.

Man was always man, and always will be, for we are the offspring of God. The fact that we know of our own form and image and the further fact that we are God's offspring give us positive knowledge of the form and image of God, after whom we are made and of whom we are born as his children.

God would not violate his own laws. When he decreed that all reproduction was to be "after its kind," he obeyed the same law. We are therefore of the race of God. To follow an opposite philosophy is to lead us into atheism.

To understand the relationship of our preexistence to our form and nature here in mortality is most important. There were two creations, as the scriptures clearly indicate, one spiritual and the other temporal. (Moses 3:5-7; Abraham 3:21-24.) In the spiritual creation the Lord made the spirits of all forms of life; in the temporal, he made mortal bodies for the spirits that he had thus created previously.

That is one of the reasons the scriptures read: "Thus the heavens and the earth were finished." The universes, of course, were made by him, but likewise in the heavens—in our preexistence with him—the spirits of all forms of life were made.

Moses, in the Bible, makes this clear as he says:

These are the *generations* of the heavens and of the earth when they were created, in the day that the Lord made the earth and the heavens, and every plant of the field *before it was in the earth,* and every herb of the field *before it grew:* for the Lord God had not caused it to rain upon the earth, and there was not a man to till the ground. (Genesis 2:4-5. Italics added.)

Remember that this was revelation to Moses.

Further meaning is given to this in section 77 of the Doctrine and Covenants. The Prophet Joseph Smith inquired of the Lord concerning the meaning of certain parts of the book of Revelation in the Bible. The Lord explained:

Q. What are we to understand by the four beasts, spoken of in the same verse?

A. They are figurative expressions, used by the Revelator, John, in describing heaven, the paradise of God, the happiness of man, and of beasts, and of creeping things, and of the fowls of the air; that which is spiritual being in the likeness of that which is temporal; and that which is temporal in the likeness of that which is spiritual; the spirit of man in the likeness of his person, as also the spirit of the beast, and every other creature which God has created. (D&C 77:2.)

The language is most interesting: "of man, and of beasts, and of creeping things, and of the fowls of the air; *that which is spiritual being in the likeness of that which is temporal; and that which is temporal in the likeness of that which is spiritual.*"

And then this: "*the spirit of man in the likeness of his person.*" This is important as we keep in mind that man was always man, since he was born of God as man in the spirit in the preexistence, and his mortal body was made to fit his spirit.

The Lord's explanation continues: "*as also the spirit of the beast, and every other creature which God has created.*"

The fact that all life was made in the spirit before there even was an earth, and that every mortal body was made to fit the spirit of that form of life as it was made in the preexistence, should answer for every believer in the revelations to Joseph Smith the question of the origin of life. God made life in all its forms. Life did not generate spontaneously, either from nothing, as the sectarians teach, or from any primeval amino acids, as scientists speculate. It was planned, ordered, and accomplished by the Divine Mind of Almighty God, our Heavenly Father, together with his most Beloved Son, the Lord Jesus Christ, our Redeemer.

Part of that planning was the appointment by the Lord of many of his outstanding spirit children who were to become his leaders after their birth into mortality.

Elder LeGrand Richards of the Council of the Twelve, writing in the February 1977 issue of the *New Era,* referred to our preexistent life. He emphasized the fact that God knew each of us in the period before the earth was formed. He knew us as individuals; he knew our talents and our capabilities. Therefore, Elder Richards explains, God, having this knowledge, chose from among his spirit children while still in the spirit world those who were to become his leaders on earth after they were born into mortality.

He said in part:

Not only Abraham was chosen before he was born, but many others of whom we have record, and the only reason they were chosen before they were born is that God knew them. He stood in their midst, the great and the noble, and of course, all of the other spirits, but this particular reference says that He stood in the midst of the great and the noble spirits.

Of all those noble spirits to come upon the earth, the most wonderful, of course, was Christ our Lord, the firstborn, the Son of God. Satan was another and, without going into details, Satan was a morning star, one of the bright spirits, but because of his own actions, he was cast down to the earth and brought with him a third of the host of heaven.

Because these spirits lived and they were known—for God knew them—all of the prophets have spoken of the work of Christ and what He would do long before he was ever born into this world. They even declared the very minutest details with respect to His life, His ministry, His crucifixion, even that men would cast lots for His raiment when He should be put to death. And all of that was possible because He was known unto God.

Let us now consider John the Baptist. You remember that the angel Gabriel appeared to Elizabeth and told her that she would bear a son and that he would be a forerunner to go before and prepare the way for the coming of the Redeemer of the world. If he had had his beginning without that spiritual existence, it would seem almost incredible to think that anybody could tell what nature of spirit was about to be born into the world.

In the words of Isaiah, "Known unto God are all of his works from the beginning." He does not have to wait to see things worked out here in mortality, because He has decreed certain things and objectives shall be achieved, and He has made preparations and provision in advance by sending certain spirits for their day and time. Their lives and their ministry [are] known to God just as much before they are born as was the mission and ministry of His only Begotten Son. That is why Gabriel could announce the coming of John and his great mission in the world.

Consider also the mission of John the Beloved, the apostle of the Lord Jesus Christ. God did not need to wait until John the Beloved had lived upon the earth in order to know what his mission was in life. John had already prepared himself in the eternal world for the great mission whereunto he was called. That is why 600 years before Christ, an angel of God could reveal to Nephi the things that John would accomplish. (Read 1 Nephi 14:20-27.) . . .

There is a marvelous promise concerning the mission of Joseph Smith, the seer and prophet "like unto Moses," that he should do no other work, save the work which the Lord should command him, and that the work that he should bring forth, by the power of God should bring many people unto salvation. (See 2 Nephi 3.) . . .

I remind you of Jeremiah who was called to be a prophet.

"Then the word of the Lord came unto me, saying, Before I formed thee in the belly I knew thee; and before thou camest forth out of the womb I sanctified thee, and I ordained thee a prophet unto the nations.

"Then said I, Ah, Lord God! behold, I cannot speak: for I am a child." (Jer. 1:4-6.) . . .

The Apostle Paul understood that the Lord called men before they were born. Here are a few verses from the first chapter of Ephesians.

"Paul, an apostle of Jesus Christ by the will of God, to the saints which are at Ephesus, and to the faithful in Christ Jesus:

"Grace be to you, and peace, from God our Father, and from the Lord Jesus Christ.

"Blessed be the God and Father of our Lord Jesus Christ, who hath blessed us with all spiritual blessings in heavenly places in Christ.

"According as he hath chosen us in him before the foundation of the world, that we should be holy and without blame before him in love." (Eph. 1:1-4.)

So you see, those whom God hath chosen before the foundation of the world—and I would like to bear my testimony to you that most of us who were born under the new and everlasting covenant, and those of us who have heeded the voice of the messengers of eternal truths and have accepted the same, come under this promise—He has called out of the world to be his leaders, to be a light unto the world.

Chapter 26

MOSES
AND SATAN

Moses confronted Satan—and won.

He challenged him face to face, and recognized him as the liar that he is, although he trembled when the devil went into a tantrum. It was a bitter experience, but Moses was victorious.

The Lord had revealed to Moses that Satan rebelled against God in the primeval council in heaven where "he became Satan, yea, even the devil, the father of all lies, to deceive and to blind men, and to lead them captive at his will, even as many as would not hearken unto my voice." (Moses 4:4.)

He further explained that Satan sought to destroy the agency of man "which I, the Lord God, had given him, and also, that I should give unto him mine own power." And then the Lord said: "By the power of mine Only Begotten, I caused that he should be cast down." (Moses 4:3.)

Thus Satan became the devil, but thus also it was demonstrated that the power of Christ is greater than the power of the devil.

When Moses saw God face to face and talked with him, the Lord allowed divine glory to rest upon the prophet, and this made it possible for him to endure the heavenly presence. (Moses 1:2.)

The great revelation that was thus given to Moses preceded what probably was the most devastating experience of his life. It was a confrontation with the devil in person. The Pearl of Great Price account is so direct and descriptive it is best reproduced as it is:

And it came to pass that when Moses had said these words, behold, Satan came tempting him, saying: Moses, son of man, worship me.

And it came to pass that Moses looked upon Satan and said: Who art thou? For behold, I am a son of God, in the similitude of his Only Begotten; and where is thy glory, that I should worship thee?

For behold, I could not look upon God, except his glory should come upon me, and I were strengthened before him. But I can look upon thee in the natural man. Is it not so, surely?

Blessed be the name of my God, for his Spirit hath not altogether withdrawn from me, or else where is thy glory, for it is darkness unto me? And I can judge between thee and God; for God said unto me: Worship God, for him only shalt thou serve.

Get thee hence, Satan; deceive me not; for God said unto me: Thou art after the similitude of mine Only Begotten.

And he also gave me commandments when he called unto me out of the burning bush, saying: Call upon God in the name of mine Only Begotten, and worship me. (Moses 1:12-17.)

Three times Moses commanded Satan to depart. It was only when he spoke in the name of the Only Begotten that Lucifer obeyed.

The scriptural account continues:

And again Moses said: I will not cease to call upon God, I have other things to inquire of him: for his glory has been upon me, wherefore I can judge between him and thee. Depart hence, Satan.

And now, when Moses had said these words, Satan cried with a loud voice, and rent upon the earth, and commanded, saying: I am the Only Begotten, worship me.

And it came to pass that Moses began to fear exceedingly; and as he began to fear, he saw the bitterness of hell. Nevertheless, calling upon God, he received strength, and he commanded, saying: Depart from me, Satan, for this one God only will I worship, which is the God of glory.

And now Satan began to tremble, and the earth shook; and Moses received strength, and called upon God, saying: In the name of the Only Begotten, depart hence, Satan.

And it came to pass that Satan cried with a loud voice, with weeping, and wailing, and gnashing of teeth; and he departed hence, even from the presence of Moses, that he beheld him not.

And now of this thing Moses bore record; but because of wickedness it is not had among the children of men. (Moses 1:18-23.)

The experience of Joseph Smith and Sidney Rigdon closely resembled that of Moses, as they also saw the devil. In what is now section 76 of the Doctrine and Covenants they first bore testimony of Christ as follows:

And while we meditated upon these things, the Lord touched the eyes of our understandings and they were opened, and the glory of the Lord shone round about.

And we beheld the glory of the Son, on the right hand of the Father, and received of his fulness;

And saw the holy angels, and them who are sanctified before his throne, worshiping God, and the Lamb, who worship him forever and ever.

And now, after the many testimonies which have been given of him, this is the testimony, last of all, which we give of him: That he lives!

For we saw him, even on the right hand of God; and we heard the voice bearing record that he is the Only Begotten of the Father—

That by him, and through him, and of him, the worlds are and were created, and the inhabitants thereof are begotten sons and daughters unto God. (D&C 76:19-24.)

Immediately following this heavenly experience they were given a view of the devil and wrote the following:

And this we saw also, and bear record, that an angel of God who was in authority in the presence of God, who rebelled against the Only Begotten Son whom the Father loved and who was in the bosom of the Father, was thrust down from the presence of God and the Son,

And was called Perdition, for the heavens wept over him—he was Lucifer, a son of the morning.

And we beheld, and lo, he is fallen! is fallen, even a son of the morning!

And while we were yet in the Spirit, the Lord commanded us that we should write the vision; for we beheld Satan, that old serpent, even the devil, who rebelled against God, and sought to take the kingdom of our God and his Christ—

Wherefore, he maketh war with the saints of God, and encompasseth them round about.

And we saw a vision of the sufferings of those with whom he made war and overcame, for thus came the voice of the Lord unto us:

Thus saith the Lord concerning all those who know my power, and have been made partakers thereof, and suffered themselves through the power of the devil to be overcome, and to deny the truth and defy my power—

They are they who are the sons of perdition, of whom I say that it had been better for them never to have been born;

For they are vessels of wrath, doomed to suffer the wrath of God, with the devil and his angels in eternity;

Concerning whom I have said there is no forgiveness in this world nor in the world to come—

Having denied the Holy Spirit after having received it, and having denied the Only Begotten Son of the Father, having crucified him unto themselves and put him to an open shame.

These are they who shall go away into the lake of fire and brimstone, with the devil and his angels—

And the only ones on whom the second death shall have any power;

Yea, verily, the only ones who shall not be redeemed in the due time of the Lord, after the sufferings of his wrath. (D&C 76:25-38.)

No one could tell either Moses or Joseph Smith that the devil was not a reality or that he was merely a mythological spook to frighten little children.

Some of the elders of the Church have likewise battled Satan and his imps. The experience of Heber C. Kimball and his missionary companions in Great Britain was one of the most frightening things to happen in this dispensation. Brother Kimball's account follows:

One Saturday evening I was appointed by the brethren to baptize a number the next morning in the River Ribble which runs through that place. By this time the adversary of souls began a rage and he felt a determination to destroy us before we had fully established the gospel in that land; and the next morning I witnessed such a scene of satanic power and influence as I shall never forget while memory lasts.

About daybreak, Brother Russell (who was appointed to preach in the marketplace that day), who slept in the second story of the house in which we were entertained, came up to the room where Elder Hyde and I were sleeping and called upon us to arise and pray for him, for he was so afflicted with evil spirits that he could not live long unless he should obtain relief.

We immediately arose, laid hands upon him and prayed that the Lord would have mercy on his servant and rebuke the devil. While thus engaged, I was struck with great force by some invisible power and fell senseless to the floor as if I had been shot, and the first thing that I recollected was, that I was supported by Brothers Hyde and Russell, who were beseeching the throne of grace in my behalf. They then laid me on the bed, but my agony was so great that I could not endure, and I was obliged to get out, and fell on my knees and began to pray. I then sat on the bed and could distinctly see the evil spirits, who foamed and gnashed their teeth upon us. We gazed upon them about an hour and a half, and I shall never forget the horror and malignity depicted on the countenances of these foul spirits, and any attempt to paint the scene which then presented itself, or portray the malice and enmity depicted in their countenances would be vain.

I perspired exceedingly, and my clothes were as wet as if I had been taken out of the river. I felt exquisite pain, and was in the greatest distress for some time. However, I learned by it the power of the adversary, his enmity against the servants of God and got some understanding of the invisible world. (Journal of Heber C. Kimball.)

Chapter 27

APOSTASY FROM THE LAW

By the time of the Savior's mortal ministry, the Israelites in Palestine had apostatized very largely from the law of Moses.

In America the law was kept among the Book of Mormon peoples even until the time of Christ, although they lived other principles of the gospel as well.

But among the residents of Palestine, a general falling away took place. So extensive was that apostasy that Jesus said at one time: "Did not Moses give you the law, and yet none of you keepeth the law? Why go ye about to kill me?" (John 7:19.)

His persecutors had in fact become murderous in their intentions, and time and again they sought to kill him, even from the early part of his ministry.

The immediate cause of Jesus' eventual crucifixion was this same religious bigotry. His true doctrines were so at variance with the teachings of the day, and so strikingly did they expose the error of the creeds then taught, that his enemies became incensed and sought his life.

When the scribes and Pharisees came to him and complained, "Why do thy disciples transgress the tradition of the elders? for they wash not their hands when they eat bread," he countered with "Why do ye also transgress the commandment of God by your tradition?" (Matthew 15:2-3.)

He told his disciples to beware of the doctrines of the Pharisees and the Sadducees (Matthew 16:1-12), calling them a wicked and adulterous generation that sought for signs. He denounced their man-made creeds and said, "In vain do they worship me, teaching for doctrines the commandments of men." (Matthew 15:9.)

The Jerusalem Bible gives this rendering of the Savior's denunciation:

"This people honours me only with lip-service, while their hearts are far from me. The worship they offer me is worthless, the doctrines they teach are only human regulations.

"You put aside the commandment of God to cling to human traditions." And he said to them, "How ingeniously you get around the commandment of God in order to preserve your own tradition! . . . you make God's word null and void for the sake of your tradition which you have handed down. And you do many other things like this." (Jerusalem Bible, Mark 7:6-13.)

The Roman Catholic adaptation of the Protestant Revised Version of the Bible, published in England in 1965, gives this for Matthew 15:3-6: "And why do you transgress the commandment of God for the sake of your tradition? . . . So for the sake of your tradition you have made void the word of God."

Jesus scathingly denounced the scribes, Pharisees, Sadducees, and other false teachers. The whole of Matthew 23 should be read in this regard. Particularly he said:

Woe unto you, scribes and Pharisees, hypocrites! for ye compass sea and land to make one proselyte, and when he is made, ye make him twofold more the child of hell than yourselves.

Woe unto you, ye blind guides, which say, Whosoever shall swear by the temple, it is nothing; but whosoever shall swear by the gold of the temple, he is a debtor!

Ye fools and blind: for whether is greater, the gold, or the temple that sanctifieth the gold?

Woe unto you, scribes and Pharisees, hypocrites! for ye pay tithe of mint and anise and cummin, and have omitted the weightier matters of the law, judgment, mercy, and faith: these ought ye to have done, and not to leave the other undone.

Ye blind guides, which strain at a gnat, and swallow a camel.

Woe unto you, scribes and Pharisees, hypocrites! for ye make clean the outside of the cup and of the platter, but within they are full of extortion and excess.

Thou blind Pharisee, cleanse first that which is within the cup and platter, that the outside of them may be clean also.

Woe unto you, scribes and Pharisees, hypocrites! for ye are like unto whited sepulchres, which indeed appear beautiful outward, but are within full of dead men's bones, and of all uncleanness.

Even so ye also outwardly appear righteous unto men, but within ye are full of hypocrisy and iniquity. (Matthew 23:15-17, 23-28.)

We see their scheming methods as we read:

And the chief priests and the scribes the same hour sought to lay hands on him; and they feared the people: for they perceived that he had spoken this parable against them.

And they watched him, and sent forth spies, which should feign themselves just men, that they might take hold of his words, that so they might deliver him unto the power and authority of the governor. (Luke 20:19-20.)

But then, out of the greatness of his heart, he said: "O Jerusalem, Jerusalem, thou that killest the prophets, and stonest them which are sent unto thee, how often would I have gathered thy children together, even as a hen gathereth her chickens under her wings, and ye would not!" (Matthew 23:37.)

The people of Palestine at that day, apostate as they were, hypocritical and posing as though they were devout, yet being murderous in their hearts, were divided into various factions or religious denominations.

The Pharisees and Sadducees are best known. The Pharisees had developed into a sect prior to the time of the Maccabees when an effort was made to force the Jews to adopt Greek customs and philosophies. They had built upon the traditions of the elders who preceded them and used them in their violent opposition to Hellenistic influences. They carried their self-written creeds to ridiculous extremes, which were exposed by the Savior. Hence they bitterly fought Jesus and became anti-Christ.

The Sadducees were organized by a man named Zadok or Sadok about 300 B.C., and were at times called Zadokites. They denied both the immortality of the soul and the resurrection, and rejected the traditions of the elders on which the Pharisees so much depended.

There were also the Essenes, who are believed to have written the Dead Sea scrolls. They were a sect of men only who believed in celibacy and taught that to be saved one must withdraw from society and live the ascetic life. They had all things in common and spent their time in meditation. They developed mystical tendencies.

There were also the Zealots, a religious-political group who opposed Roman rule in Palestine, but who objected to many of the teachings of the Pharisees and the Sadducees.

Then there were the Hellenists, who were a residue of the Greek attempt to Hellenize the world following the conquests of Alexander the Great.

Alexander and his successors, in order to solidify their empire, sent groups of Greeks as colonists to various parts of their new domain, including Palestine. These Greeks introduced many of their cultural activities, including the Greek games, wherever they were thus transplanted by their emperors.

As they endeavored to Hellenize the Jews in this way, they met great resistance, which culminated in the wars of the Maccabees. The Hellenist party attempted to dilute the Mosaic teachings with Greek philosophy, and to a considerable extent they were successful among certain groups. King Herod the Great encouraged them.

So influential upon Jewry was Greek culture in those days, and so extensively was it adopted by the Romans when they came into power, that the Old Testament was translated into Greek. This work was known as the Septuagint and was done in Alexandria between 280 and 130 B.C. It was this same Greek influence in early Christian times that made it necessary for the New Testament also to be made available in Greek.

The Hellenist party, as it was known, invaded Christianity also. It was a minority group until the Roman conquest of Jerusalem in A.D. 70. Since Hellenism was encouraged by the Romans, who dearly loved Greek culture, believing it was better than their own, the Hellenists were not scattered at the fall of Jerusalem as were most of the other Christian sects. Thus they became the dominant though splintered cult of early Christianity. Eventually this was the sect that was sponsored by Constantine the Great.

Many Christian sects arose immediately after Christ. Some historians say that as many as thirty appeared within the first century. These included the Judeo-Christians, who tried to Judaize Christian teachings; the Millenarianists; the Encratites; the Ebionites; the Gnostics; the Elkasaites (known as baptists); the Archontics; the Coptics, who still survive in Egypt; the Mandaeans; the Manichaeans; and the Quartodecimans.

It is readily seen that it is a great mistake to suppose there was only one united Christian church until the rupture that formed the Greek Orthodox Church a thousand years after Christ.

There was no unity in early Christianity; the church was splintered time and again, thus making it impossible truthfully or accurately to trace any one denomination back to either Peter or Christ. The original church was lost in the splintering process that took place, beginning even in the days of the apostles. See the first chapter of I Corinthians, for example, where four factions were mentioned in that one city.

Do we remember how Paul wrote to the Galatians and marveled that they had so soon left the true faith (Galatians 1:6-9) and how he called them "O foolish Galatians . . . . that ye should not obey the truth" (Galatians 3:1)? This was but typical of the ruptures that began in the days of the apostles.

But to return to the situation during the life of Christ: It should be remembered that the various cults that existed then, all of them apostate, all with their own separate creeds, wrote voluminous instructions on how to live various portions of the law of Moses. These rules became traditions of the elders and even found their way into such works as the Talmud.

In the old Jerusalem Talmud alone there were sixty-five printed columns explaining how to observe the Sabbath. Among a few of them were:

A man may not go out on the Sabbath with sandals shod with nails. The nails constitute a burden and to carry a burden on the Sabbath is a violation of the law.

A man might not cut his finger nails on the Sabbath, nor pull a hair out of his beard or head.

If one extinguished a lamp on the Sabbath he broke the law.

It was forbidden to ask a doctor to assist one on the Sabbath. To set a broken bone was against the law. If a hand or foot were dislocated it was against the law to do anything but bathe it in the usual way.

To tie a knot on the Sabbath was work and therefore forbidden, unless to tie or untie the knot could be accomplished with only one hand. If it could be done with one hand it did not violate the law.

These are but typical of the false man-made creeds of that day. And yet those people, apparently so pious, were willing to commit murder and slay the Savior because he healed on the Sabbath! (John 5:16.) So apostate were they.

Nephi wrote of them:

> Wherefore, as I said unto you, it must needs be expedient that Christ—for in the last night the angel spake unto me that this should be his name—should come among the Jews, among those who are the more wicked part of the world; and they shall crucify him—for thus it behooveth our God, and there is none other nation on earth that would crucify their God.
>
> For should the mighty miracles be wrought among other nations they would repent, and know that he be their God.
>
> But because of priestcrafts and iniquities, they at Jerusalem will stiffen their necks against him, that he be crucified. (2 Nephi 10:3-5.)

This is even more significant when we read what the Lord said to Enoch: "Wherefore, I can stretch forth mine hands and hold all the creations which I have made; and mine eye can pierce them also, and among all the workmanship of mine hands there has not been so great wickedness as among thy brethren." (Moses 7:36.)

There is much room for contemplation when we realize that the faithless of Enoch's day were the most wicked of all the people in God's creations and that those in Palestine in the time of Christ were the most wicked on this earth, none other being so bad that they would crucify their King.

There are many earths that are inhabited, and upon them live other sons and daughters of God. (D&C 76:24.)

Chapter 28

THE LOST OPPORTUNITY

The Lord promised the Twelve Tribes that if they would keep his commandments, he would make them the greatest nation on earth.

What an opportunity was theirs! How history would have been changed if only they had kept the faith!

In addressing the congregation Moses said: "And it shall come to pass, if thou shalt hearken diligently unto the voice of the Lord thy God, to observe and to do all his commandments which I command thee this day, that the Lord thy God will set thee on high *above all nations of the earth.*" (Deuteronomy 28:1. Italics added.)

Earlier the prophet had said:

Thou shalt therefore keep the commandments, and the statutes, and the judgments, which I command thee this day, to do them.

Wherefore it shall come to pass, if ye hearken to these judgments, and keep, and do them, that the Lord thy God shall keep unto thee the covenant and the mercy which he sware unto thy fathers:

And he will love thee, and bless thee, and multiply thee: he will also bless the fruit of thy womb, and the fruit of thy land, thy corn, and thy wine, and thine oil, the increase of thy kine, and the flocks of thy sheep, in the land which he sware unto thy fathers to give thee.

Thou shalt be *blessed above all people:* there shall not be male or female barren among you, or among your cattle.

And the Lord will take away from thee all sickness, and will put none of the evil diseases of Egypt, which thou knowest, upon thee; but will lay them upon all them that hate thee.

And thou shalt consume all the people which the Lord thy God shall deliver thee; thine eye shall have no pity upon them: neither shalt thou serve their gods; for that will be a snare unto thee.

If thou shalt say in thine heart, These nations are more than I; how can I dispossess them?

Thou shalt not be afraid of them: but shalt well remember what the Lord thy God did unto Pharaoh, and unto all Egypt;

The great temptations which thine eyes saw, and the signs, and the wonders, and the mighty hand, and the stretched out arm, whereby the Lord thy God brought thee out: so shall the Lord thy God do unto all the people of whom thou art afraid.

Moreover the Lord thy God will send the hornet among them, until they that are left, and hide themselves from thee, be destroyed.

Thou shalt not be afrighted at them: for the Lord thy God is among you, a mighty God and terrible.

And the Lord thy God will put out those nations before thee by little and little: thou mayest not consume them at once, lest the beasts of the field increase upon thee.

But the Lord thy God shall deliver them unto thee, and shall destroy them with a mighty destruction, until they be destroyed.

And he shall deliver their kings into thine hand, and thou shalt destroy their name from under heaven: there shall no man be able to stand before thee, until thou have destroyed them. (Deuteronomy 7:11-24. Italics added.)

Clearly setting forth what the Lord had in mind for Israel are these verses:

This day the Lord thy God hath commanded thee to do these statutes and judgments: thou shalt therefore keep and do them with all thine heart, and with all thy soul.

Thou hast avouched the Lord this day to be thy God, and to walk in his ways, and to keep his statutes, and his commandments, and his judgments, and to hearken unto his voice:

And the Lord hath avouched thee this day to be his peculiar people, as he hath promised thee, and that thou shouldest keep all his commandments;

And to *make thee high above all nations* which he hath made, in praise, and in name, and in honour; and that thou mayest be an holy people unto the Lord thy God, as he hath spoken. (Deuteronomy 26:16-19. Italics added.)

There were great nations in those times, and some of them continued on down until as late as 600 B.C. Sargon I created one of the greatest of the ancient nations (2300 B.C.) in Mesopotamia. He conquered all the nearby lands and then extended his empire as far as present-day Syria and Turkey. About a dozen kings paid him tribute.

He built his capital at Agade, regarded as one of the most magnificent cities of antiquity, with its great temples and spectacular royal palace, resplendent with treasures from all parts of his empire.

Under one of his successors, Ur-Nammu, who ruled about 2100 B.C., the nation prospered and developed remarkably. "Agriculture and commerce . . . enjoyed a dramatic upswing, and in all branches of the arts there occurred a sudden renaissance." (*Cradle of Civilization,* p. 39.)

Ur-Nammu is considered by historians to be the first known law-giver in history. "His law code, parts of which have been found inscribed on cuneiform tablets, preceded the celebrated code of Hammurabi by more than three centuries and the laws of Moses by over a millennium." (Ibid., p. 40.)

And consider Hammurabi himself. He ascended the throne of Babylon about 1750 B.C., but a few short years before Joseph was sold into Egypt. His nation had been great for two hundred years prior to the time of Abraham.

The art and architecture of those people were kept on a high plane for five hundred years. The Babylonians were truly a great nation. Hammurabi's Code of Laws is regarded as one of the marvels of that ancient time.

One of the truly remarkable civilizations of ancient times was that of the Minoans on the island of Crete. They had a well-advanced culture, which has been appreciated fully only recently, since more archaeological discoveries have been made.

The Egyptians remained outstanding all through the centuries, beginning at about 3000 B.C. The Elamites, spoken of in the Bible, were no insignificant power either.

The Assyrians appeared about 1800 B.C. shortly after Abraham's time, only about a century before Joseph was sold into Egypt. They continued to be a power to be reckoned with for twelve hundred years. The Hittites too reached considerable heights for about four hundred years beginning about 1700 B.C.

Should we not mention the Jaredites in America, who lived during these same periods? Their records certainly show them to have been advanced. The book of Ether gives testimony to this.

One of the greatest of the ancient nations, but more recent than some of these, was Greece, whose influence is still with us.

Through archaeology it has been discovered that these nations were of far greater importance than previously realized. Most of them were strong military powers, but with all their skills in war, they also had cultural activities without which no nation can be great.

And the Israelites could have been greater than them all! If they had lived up to their opportunity, the entire course of history could have been changed. The Lord's miracles in their behalf, and the prosperity with which he would have blessed them, would have more than guaranteed their complete superiority.

In Leviticus (26:6) they were promised peace and safety and "neither shall the sword go through your land."

This was a notable promise, for history shows that Palestine became the battleground not only for the Israelites, but also for other warring nations, north and south, which trampled over the area in repeated campaigns. If only the sword had not gone through their land!

It is true that in the days of Solomon the tribes became a great and rich nation, attracting even the Queen of Sheba to Palestine. But although the nation reached a partial peak at that time, it did not even approach what the Lord had in mind. By disobedience it was all lost to internal conflict, civil war, and invasion.

The Ten Tribes were lost in exile. The remaining two tribes suffered their Babylonian captivity and were later sifted over the earth.

In calling them to repentance, the Lord said that unless they turned from their wickedness, "I will walk contrary unto you also in fury; . . . And I will bring the land into desolation. . . . And I will scatter you among the heathen, and will draw out a sword after you: and your land shall be desolate, and your cities waste." (Leviticus 26:28, 32-33.)

The price of disobedience is stupendous.

The Lord also said to them:

But it shall come to pass, if thou wilt not hearken unto the voice of the Lord thy God, to observe to do all his commandments and his statutes which I command thee this day; that all these curses shall come upon thee, and overtake thee:
Cursed shalt thou be in the city, and cursed shalt thou be in the field.
Cursed shall be thy basket and thy store.
Cursed shall be the fruit of thy body, and the fruit of thy land, the increase of thy kine, and the flocks of thy sheep.
Cursed shalt thou be when thou comest in, and cursed shalt thou be when thou goest out.
The Lord shall send upon thee cursing, vexation, and rebuke, in all

that thou settest thine hand unto for to do, until thou be destroyed, and until thou perish quickly; because of the wickedness of thy doings, whereby thou hast forsaken me.

The Lord shall make the pestilence cleave unto thee, until he have consumed thee from off the land, whither thou goest to possess it.

The Lord shall smite thee with a consumption, and with a fever, and with an inflammation, and with an extreme burning, and with the sword, and with blasting, and with mildew; and they shall pursue thee until thou perish.

And thy heaven that is over thy head shall be brass, and the earth that is under thee shall be iron.

The Lord shall make the rain of thy land powder and dust: from heaven shall it come down upon thee, until thou be destroyed.

The Lord shall cause thee to be smitten before thine enemies: thou shalt go out one way against them, and flee seven ways before them: and shalt be removed into all the kingdoms of the earth.

And thy carcase shall be meat unto all fowls of the air, and unto the beasts of the earth, and no man shall fray them away.

The Lord will smite thee with the botch of Egypt, and with the emerods, and with the scab, and with the itch, whereof thou canst not be healed.

The Lord shall smite thee with madness, and blindness, and astonishment of heart:

And thou shalt grope at noonday, as the blind gropeth in darkness, and thou shalt not prosper in thy ways: and thou shalt be only oppressed and spoiled evermore, and no man shall save thee.

Thou shalt betroth a wife, and another man shall lie with her: thou shalt build an house, and thou shalt not dwell therein: thou shalt plant a vineyard, and shalt not gather the grapes thereof.

Thine ox shall be slain before thine eyes, and thou shalt not eat thereof: thine ass shall be violently taken away from before thy face, and shall not be restored to thee: thy sheep shall be given unto thine enemies, and thou shalt have none to rescue them.

Thy sons and thy daughters shall be given unto another people, and thine eyes shall look, and fail with longing for them all the day long: and there shall be no might in thine hand.

The fruit of thy land, and all thy labours, shall a nation which thou knowest not eat up; and thou shalt be only oppressed and crushed alway:

So that thou shalt be mad for the sight of thine eyes which thou shalt see.

The Lord shall smite thee in the knees, and in the legs, with a sore botch that cannot be healed, from the sole of thy foot unto the top of thy head.

The Lord shall bring thee, and thy king which thou shalt set over thee, unto a nation which neither thou nor thy fathers have known; and there shalt thou serve other gods, wood and stone.

And thou shalt become an astonishment, a proverb, and a byword, among all nations whither the Lord shall lead thee.

Thou shalt carry much seed out into the field, and shalt gather but little in; for the locust shall consume it.

Thou shalt plant vineyards, and dress them, but shalt neither drink of the wine, nor gather the grapes; for the worms shall eat them.

Thou shalt have olive trees throughout all thy coasts, but thou shalt not anoint thyself with the oil; for thine olive shall cast his fruit.

Thou shalt beget sons and daughters, but thou shalt not enjoy them; for they shall go into captivity.

All thy trees and fruit of thy land shall the locust consume.

The stranger that is within thee shall get up above thee very high; and thou shalt come down very low.

He shall lend to thee, and thou shalt not lend to him: he shall be the head, and thou shalt be the tail.

Moreover all these curses shall come upon thee, and shall pursue thee, and overtake thee, til thou be destroyed; because thou hearkenedst not unto the voice of the Lord thy God, to keep his commandments and his statutes which he commanded thee:

And they shall be upon thee for a sign and for a wonder, and upon thy seed for ever.

Because thou servedst not the Lord thy God with joyfulness, and with gladness of heart, for the abundance of all things;

Therefore shalt thou serve thine enemies which the Lord shall send against thee, in hunger, and in thirst, and in nakedness, and in want of all things: and he shall put a yoke of iron upon thy neck, until he have destroyed thee.

The Lord shall bring a nation against thee from far, from the end of the earth, as swift as the eagle flieth; a nation whose tongue thou shalt not understand;

A nation of fierce countenance, which shall not regard the person of the old, nor shew favour to the young:

And he shall eat the fruit of thy cattle, and the fruit of thy land, until thou be destroyed: which also shall not leave thee either corn, wine, or oil, or the increase of thy kine, or flocks of thy sheep, until he have destroyed thee.

And he shall besiege thee in all thy gates, until thy high and fenced walls come down, wherein thou trustedst, throughout all thy land: and he shall besiege thee in all thy gates throughout all thy land, which the Lord thy God hath given thee. (Deuteronomy 28:15-52.)

The curse went on still further, as may be seen by reading to the end of Deuteronomy 28.

The basic problem was that the Israelites, although the covenant people, really had little or no genuine faith in God. The Lord had tried so hard to demonstrate his own reality and his love for them; he had reminded them over and over of his covenant with Abraham, and his obligation, under that covenant, to bless them and prosper them—and his great desire to do so—if only they would obey him. But they did not believe and did not repent; they killed the prophets who warned them of impending doom, and indulged in the sins of the world. Their sins loomed greater in the eyes of God because they were so blatantly violating their sacred covenants.

They wanted so much to be like other nations, and not become the peculiar people the Lord had in mind. This "peculiar" status would have made them happy, clean, upright, prosperous, and spiritual in the true sense; the greatest nation on earth.

A notable expression of the same philosophy that lost them their privileged inheritance was observed when they clamored to the prophet Samuel for a king "like the other nations." They had been told repeatedly how wicked those nations were, and yet they wanted to be like them.

The entire drama of ancient Israel was a tragedy of tremendous proportions, a bitter lesson in disobedience. And how similar it was to the history of the Nephites in America, and their eventual destruction!

And why? Because the Lord cannot look upon sin with the least degree of allowance.

Chapter 29

THE DEATH OF MOSES

Did Moses die, or was he translated?

After Moses had completed his work and had brought the Twelve Tribes to the borders of the Promised Land, he climbed "the mountain of Nebo, to the top of Pisgah" and the Lord "shewed him all the land of Gilead, unto Dan."

And the Lord said: "This is the land which I sware unto Abraham, unto Isaac, and unto Jacob, saying, I will give it unto thy seed."

But then the Lord added:

I have caused thee to see it with thine eyes, but thou shalt not go over thither.

So Moses the servant of the Lord died there in the land of Moab, according to the word of the Lord.

And he buried him in a valley in the land of Moab, over against Bethpeor: but no man knoweth of his sepulchre unto this day.

And Moses was an hundred and twenty years old when he died: his eye was not dim, nor his natural force abated.

And the children of Israel wept for Moses in the plains of Moab thirty days: so the days of weeping and mourning for Moses were ended. (Deuteronomy 34:1-8.)

In the first chapter of Joshua, who was appointed as Moses' successor, we read:

Now after the death of Moses the servant of the Lord it came to pass, that the Lord spake unto Joshua the son of Nun, Moses' minister, saying,

Moses my servant is dead; now therefore arise, go over this Jordan, thou, and all this people, unto the land which I do give to them, even to the children of Israel. (Joshua 1:1-2.)

A puzzling scripture occurs in Jude, where we read: "Yet Michael the archangel, when contending with the devil he disputed about the body of Moses." (Jude 9.)

And then we have this from the Book of Mormon:

And when Alma had done this he departed out of the land of Zarahemla, as if to go into the land of Melek. And it came to pass that he was never heard of more; as to his death or burial we know not of.

Behold, this we know, that he was a righteous man; and the saying went abroad in the church that he was taken up by the Spirit, or buried by the hand of the Lord, even as Moses. *But behold, the scriptures saith the Lord took Moses unto himself; and we suppose that he has also received Alma in the spirit, unto himself;* therefore, for this cause we know nothing concerning his death and burial. (Alma 45:18-19. Italics added.)

President Joseph Fielding Smith discussed this matter and said:

Now, there was a *reason* for the translation of Elijah. *Men are not preserved in that manner unless there is a reason for it.* Moses was likewise taken up, though the scriptures say that the Lord buried him upon the mountain. Of course, the writer of that wrote according to his understanding; but *Moses, like Elijah, was taken up without tasting death, because he had a mission to perform. . . .*

When Moses and Elijah came to the Savior and to Peter, James, and John upon the Mount, what was their coming for? Was it just some spiritual manifestation to strengthen these three apostles? Or did they come merely to give comfort unto the Son of God in his ministry and to prepare him for his crucifixion? No! That was not the purpose. I will read it to you. The Prophet Joseph Smith has explained it as follows:

"The priesthood is everlasting. *The Savior, Moses, and Elias (Elijah, in other words) gave the keys to Peter, James, and John, on the Mount when they were transfigured before him.* The priesthood is everlasting—without beginning of days or end of years; without father, mother, etc. If there is no change of ordinances, there is no change of priesthood. Wherever the ordinances of the gospel are administered, there is the priesthood. . . ."

From that we understand why Elijah and Moses were preserved from death: because *they had a mission to perform,* and it had to be performed *before* the crucifixion of the Son of God, and *it could not be done in the spirit.*

They had to have tangible bodies. Christ is the first fruits of the resurrection; therefore if any former prophets had a work to perform preparatory to the mission of the Son of God, or to the dispensation of the meridian of times, it was essential that they be preserved to fulfill that mission *in the flesh.* For that reason *Moses disappeared* from among the people and was taken up into the mountain, and the people *thought* he was buried by the Lord.

The Lord preserved him, so that he could come at the proper time and *restore his keys,* on the heads of Peter, James, and John, who stood at the head of the dispensation of the meridian of time.

He reserved Elijah from death that he might also come and bestow his keys upon the heads of Peter, James, and John and prepare them for their ministry.

But, one says, the Lord could have waited until after his resurrection, and then they could have done it. It is quite evident, due to the fact that it did so occur, that it had to be done before; and there was a reason. There may have been other reasons, but that is one reason why *Moses and Elijah did not suffer death in the flesh, like other men do.* (*Doctrines of Salvation,* Bookcraft, 1955, 1:107-11. Italics in original.)

Chapter 30

MOSES AND JOSEPH SMITH

Moses was given the keys of the gathering of Israel inasmuch as he was to bring the Twelve Tribes out of Egypt and settle them in their Promised Land.

A gathering of Israel was to be an important part of the Church in these last days also, but to accomplish this the authority to do so was required.

As the Lord sent John the Baptist to restore the Aaronic Priesthood in our day, and Peter, James, and John to restore the Melchizedek Priesthood, so he also sent others with particular keys in the priesthood.

The Prophet Joseph wrote about the bestowal of these various keys in section 128 of the Doctrine and Covenants. Among other things he said: "And the voice of Michael, the archangel; the voice of Gabriel, and of Raphael, and of divers angels, from Michael or Adam down to the present time, all declaring their dispensation, their rights, their keys, their honors, their majesty and glory, and the power of their priesthood; giving line upon line, precept upon precept. . . ." (V. 21.)

In section 110, we read of Elijah, Elias, and Moses coming to the Prophet Joseph Smith and Oliver Cowdery, bestowing the powers of their ministry for our use in this the dispensation of the fulness of times.

It is remembered that Peter had said concerning the restoration of the gospel: "And he shall send Jesus Christ, which before was preached unto you: Whom the heaven must receive until the times of restitution of all things, which God had spoken by the mouth of all his holy prophets since the world began." (Acts 3:20-21.)

Hence, all things spoken of by all the holy prophets from

the beginning of the world were destined to be restored as part of this last dispensation.

Concerning the coming of Moses the Prophet Joseph said: "After this vision closed, the heavens were again opened unto us; and Moses appeared before us, and committed unto us the keys of the gathering of Israel from the four parts of the earth, and the leading of the ten tribes from the land of the north." (D&C 110:11.)

There was a notable gathering of the Saints early in the history of the Church. As converts were made, they gathered together to bolster their faith and advance the new work.

They gathered to build the temple in Kirtland, which was commanded of God. They likewise gathered to Jackson County, Missouri, in preparation for the establishment of Zion at that time. They expected to build temples at both Independence and Far West, but were driven away by their enemies.

They were gathered at Nauvoo next, primarily to build a temple of the Lord. With this in mind, the Prophet Joseph said:

> The main object [of the gathering] was to build unto the Lord a house whereby He could reveal unto His people the ordinances of his house and the glories of His kingdom, and teach the people the way of salvation; for there are certain ordinances and principles that, when they are taught and practiced, must be done in a place or house built for that purpose.
>
> It was the design of the councils of heaven before the world was, that the principles and laws of the priesthood should be predicated upon the gathering of the people in every age of the world.
>
> Jesus did everything to gather the people, and they would not be gathered, and He therefore poured out curses upon them. Ordinances instituted in the heavens before the foundation of the world, in the priesthood, for the salvation of men, are not to be altered or changed. All must be saved on the same principles.
>
> It is for the same purpose that God gathers together His people in the last days, to build unto the Lord a house to prepare them for the ordinances and endowments, washings and anointings, etc. (*Teachings of the Prophet Joseph Smith,* p. 308.)

One of the greatest gathering movements was that to the Great Basin with headquarters on the shores of the Great Salt Lake. From 1847 to 1869, when the railroad was completed, 80,000 pioneers came to Utah. From there they spread throughout the American West.

In Utah they immediately began construction of four temples for these same sacred ordinances.

Judah must be gathered to Palestine, where a holy temple will be built in the due time of the Lord. (*Teachings,* p. 286.)

Now that temples are being built in various parts of the world, these sacred structures become points of gathering for people in their respective lands in the sense in which the Prophet said:

> The Saints have not too much time to save and redeem their dead, and gather together their living relatives, that they may be saved also, before the earth will be smitten, and the consumption decreed falls upon the world.
>
> I would advise all the Saints to go to with their might and gather together all their living relatives to this place [where the temple is located], that they may be sealed and saved. (*Teachings,* p. 330.)

The construction of temples in various parts of the world is a great blessing to the Saints, who may find it convenient to gather their families in temple excursions to the temples to which they are assigned and perform the sacred work the Prophet describes.

There probably will be still other gatherings of the Saints for special purposes, such as the building of the New Jerusalem when that time comes. But all gathering will be done under the powers that Moses transmitted to the presidency of the Church, so that everything will be in proper order.

The keys of gathering were transmitted to the Prophet Joseph by Moses, and by him to his successors as each has come into the First Presidency of the Church.

It is all a part of the dispensation of the fulness of times.

Chapter 31

MAN OF MIRACLES

The greatest miracle of Moses' life was the fact of his intimate relationship with God. He enjoyed an actual companionship with the Almighty, and out of that close association, he gave us his unreserved testimony concerning Deity.

He knew God lives, because he saw him, talked with him, argued with him, was rebuked of him, and was sustained by him. He stood in the presence of the Lord. He received revelations and commandments without parallel.

Modern scripture gives to Moses the status that belongs to him:

A friend of God.

A companion to God.

A revelator for God.

An inspired leader of the people of God.

A writer of sacred history testifying of God.

Moses' life is a study in obedience to the divine will. The meekest of all men, he was completely dedicated to the Lord. But even so, at least on one occasion he forgot his humility as he struck the rock and commanded the water to come forth.

God taught him a great lesson in that experience, and as a result forbade him admittance to the Promised Land. What a disappointment it must have been to Moses! But how vital it was for him, and for all mankind, to learn that "without me ye can do nothing"! (John 15:5.)

In all things, as Moses obeyed, God not only blessed him but also honored him, magnified him before the people, upheld him before Pharaoh, and allowed him to be the instrument through whom he performed miracle after miracle, a seemingly endless display of divine power.

Under the leadership of Moses, the Lord fed the people, blessed them that their clothing did not wear out in forty years, gave them irresistible testimonies of his presence, and laid down laws of successful behavior which, if followed, would have made Israel the greatest nation on earth.

Modern scripture is our great reservoir of sustaining knowledge concerning Moses, but now even the scholars are beginning to credit him for what he did.

For example, Dr. Robert Young, author of the *Analytical Concordance to the Bible,* gives Moses his proper dues in this way:

He was skilled in all the wisdom of the Egyptians. His patriotic desire for his brethren at last compelled him to leave Egypt when forty years of age, to which he returned after an interval of forty years' sojourn in Midian only at the repeated command of God.

His successive interviews with his brethren, and with the king of Egypt, his wonderful miracles and the admirable patience, faith, and skill he evinced throughout his whole career, are graphically depicted in his works that remain. . . .

His authorship of Exodus, Leviticus, Numbers, and Deuteronomy are attested by every possible mark of an internal and of an external kind. These books bear incontestable evidence that they were composed in a wilderness state, yet with an express view to a speedy settlement in a fruitful land. . . .

As a historian, an orator, a leader, a statesman, a legislator, a patriot, and a man, Moses stands pre-eminent. But no mere genius could have made him the originator of sound jurisprudence—the great teacher of monotheism and sound morality—except he had also been a prophet of the Most High, supernaturally guided and aided in his work. (New York: Funk & Wagnall, 1911, p. 670.)

As was said of the Prophet Joseph Smith, the head of our dispensation, so it may be said appropriately of Moses, the head of his dispensation: "He lived great, and he died great in the eyes of God and his people." (D&C 135:3.) His memory will endure as it has in the past, throughout the ages.

The Savior testified of Moses, and Moses testified of the Savior. The Savior was God, and Moses was one of his greatest prophets.

INDEX

Aaron: received the priesthood, 91; called to assist Moses, 95; and sons called to serve as priests, 96; renderings of call of, 96

Aaronic Priesthood, 92-93

Abel, 152

Abinadi, 150

Aborigines in world today, 9-10

Abortion, 120

Abraham, 2-4, 7, 159

Adam, 8, 55

Adultery, 120-22, 133-35

Aged, 133

Ahmosis, Egyptian king, 18

Alexander the Great, 174

Alma, people of, 82

Almighty came to Moses on mount Sinai, 105-6, 107, 108. *See also* Christ; God; Jehovah; Lord; Savior

America, ancient, 4-7

American Book of Indians, 6

Americans, ancient, 4-5, 5-6

America's Ancient Civilizations, 5

Amulek, 25

Analytical Concordance to the Bible, 190

Ancient man: myths about, 1; intelligence of, 2; civilization of, in Ur, 2-4; civilization of, in ancient America, 4-7

Animals in exodus, 81

Apocrypha and Pseudepigrapha of the Old Testament, 47

Archaeology reversing claims about ancient man, 1

Asenath, 18

"Assumption of Moses," 47-48

Assyrians, 179

Astronomers, 53

Atonement, 72, 73-74, 115

Augur, Helen, quotation concerning ancient calendar, 5

Authentic New Testament, 98

Betrayal of Christ, 75

Bible: claims about, being reversed, 1, 2; modern translations of, 64; census figures of Israel in, 84. *See also* Scriptures

Bible and Evolution, Evidence of History and Science, 162

Bible As History, 6, 16, 17, 21

Bible Comes Alive, 1, 39, 40, 41, 64

Bible Companion, 21, 63, 82, 86

Bible Dictionary, 41

Blood of lamb at Passover, 73

Book of Jewish Knowledge, 76

Book of Mormon: civilization of people in, 5-6; tells of Joseph in Egypt, 23-24; accounts of exodus in, 86-88; reality of, 105; speaks of Moses, 145-47. *See also* Scriptures

Book of Moses given by revelation, 49

Brass plates, 24, 145-47

Caiger, Stephen L., quotation concerning monument in Egypt, 64

Cain, 55

Canaan, 4